COLLECTION MANAGEMENT

Women of Achievement

Joan of Arc

Women of Achievement

Abigail Adams
Susan B. Anthony
Tyra Banks
Clara Barton
Hillary Rodham Clinton
Marie Curie
Ellen DeGeneres
Diana, Princess of Wales
Tina Fey
Ruth Bader Ginsburg
Joan of Arc
Helen Keller
Madonna
Michelle Obama
Sandra Day O'Connor
Georgia O'Keeffe
Nancy Pelosi
Rachael Ray
Anita Roddick
Eleanor Roosevelt
Martha Stewart
Barbara Walters
Venus and Serena Williams

Women of Achievement

Joan of Arc

RELIGIOUS AND MILITARY LEADER

Janet Hubbard-Brown

CHELSEA HOUSE
PUBLISHERS
An imprint of Infobase Publishing

JOAN OF ARC

Chelsea House
An imprint of Infobase Publishing
132 West 31st Street
New York, NY 10001

Library of Congress Cataloging-in-Publication Data
Hubbard-Brown, Janet.
Joan of Arc : religious and military leader / Janet Hubbard-Brown.
p. cm. — (Women of achievement)
Includes bibliographical references and index.
ISBN 978-1-60413-710-1 (hardcover : acid-free paper) 1. Joan, of Arc, Saint, 1412–1431—Juvenile literature. 2. Christian women saints—France—Biography—Juvenile literature. 3. France—History—Charles VII, 1422–1461—Juvenile literature. I. Title. II. Series.

DC103.5.H83 2010
944'.026092—dc22
[B]
                                   2009051336

Text design by Erik Lindstrom
Cover design by Ben Peterson
Composition by EJB Publishing Services
Cover printed by Bang Printing, Brainerd, Minn.
Book printed and bound by Bang Printing, Brainerd, Minn.
Date printed: September 2010
Printed in the United States of America
10 9 8 7 6 5 4 3 2 1

This book is printed on acid-free paper.

All links and Web addresses were checked and verified to be correct at the time of publication. Because of the dynamic nature of the Web, some addresses and links may have changed since publication and may no longer be valid.

CONTENTS

A Coronation That Changed History

On July 14, 1429, a young woman wearing a white silk tunic over body armor stood beside Charles VII, the dauphin, or crown prince, of France, as he waited to be crowned king in the national cathedral of France in Reims. The reputation of the 19-year-old woman, called Joan the Maid by the French people, had preceded her. In the role of an appointed knight of the king, she had won a major victory against the English at Orleans two months earlier, after which she and the king's soldiers conquered every town between there and Reims. To the many French citizens witnessing it, the coronation was a miracle.

Joan and Charles, though worlds apart in terms of class and culture, had both been born into an environment of warfare and chaos. France and England had been fighting for many years by the time Joan was born. Today, historians refer to this period as the Hundred Years' War. In 1429, the year Joan had beaten the English at Orleans, the English were on the verge of victory, which meant that the kingdom of France would become a part of the English empire. To make matters worse, a civil war was raging between the Burgundians of France, who had sided with England, and the Armagnacs, who were fighting to keep France a separate country. Joan's village was fiercely loyal to the Armagnacs and to their king, Charles.

In 1421, two descendants of royalty had been proclaimed king of France—one from England, Henry VI, who was an infant at the time, and the other the crown prince Charles, who was then 19. At the same time, three men were claiming to be pope of the Catholic Church—one in Avignon, France, another in Rome, and a third in Spain. For centuries, the pope and the clergy, all highly educated, not only had a spiritual influence on the followers of the church, but also held tremendous political power throughout much of Europe.

Though crowning the French king in Reims adhered to tradition, the coronation itself was quite unusual because of Joan's presence. It was out of the ordinary for a woman to be present, let alone be a commoner. She was standing where a priest would normally stand. She held her standard, the only one unfurled, beside her. The white flag, 3 feet (0.9 meters) high and 12 feet (3.66 m) long, was made from a material similar to canvas and was decorated with raised lilies around the edges, a process called embossing. A figure of Jesus Christ was painted in the center, with an angel holding a fleur-de-lis, or lily. On the reverse side was an azure blue shield and two angels holding a dove. The dove held a scroll in its beak with the words *de par le Roi de Ciel* (of the party of the king of Heaven) written on it. When asked later why she had left

An engraving showing Joan of Arc *(standing with sword and flag)* at the coronation of Charles VII as king of France in 1429. The teenage girl heard voices urging her to aid Charles and save France from conquest by the English during the Hundred Years' War.

her banner open during the ceremony, Joan answered, "It had borne the burden, and it was right that it should have the honor."[1]

The coronation was also unusual in that the crown prince and his followers were in enemy territory. The citizens of Reims had—up until the arrival of the dauphin's party in their city—supported the English and the Burgundians, yet they showed little resistance when the French heir made his entrance. Because of divided loyalties among the 12 nobles and clerics who were normally in attendance at coronations, some of the most important authorities, both civil and religious, were missing.

The Duke of Burgundy, a sworn enemy of Charles, and the archbishop of Beauvais, Pierre Cauchon, were two who refused to attend. Cauchon carried a special animosity toward the girl who was being hailed as the savior of France. Because of her actions, he had been forced out of his position as archbishop of Beauvais. Moreover, he was firmly on the side of the English. In 1420, he had been one of the signers of the Treaty of Troyes, which had determined that the infant Henry VI of England would be crowned king of both countries when he came of age. The young woman who would come to be known as Joan of Arc had put a wrench into his plans. She did not know the intensity of Cauchon's feelings, but she was intuitively aware of the symbolic value of having the French king crowned at Reims in her war-torn country. It would cast the young Henry VI of England into the shadows.

Joan's supreme confidence had little to do with her personal accomplishments. In her mind, her success was God's will. Still, she was human, and as she stood beside her king, she looked out at the masses gathered to witness the coronation—her parents, cousin, and two brothers among them—she reflected upon her personal journey. Since the age of 13, she believed that she heard the voices of saints. At first she had been frightened, but eventually she came to think of it as a calling, a miracle. The voices had led her to a meeting with the crown prince when she was 16 or 17, where she had persuaded him that her mission—to end the English siege at Orleans and to lead him to Reims for his coronation—was divinely inspired.

Town criers had announced news of the coronation as the king and his army conquered one town after another on the way to the celebration, and on the big day the Cathedral of Notre-Dame de Reims was packed. Even then the cathedral, with its high arches over the nave reaching tremendous heights, was considered an architectural wonder. More than 2,000 statues adorned the interior and exterior of the building. The stained glass, especially the circular rose window, was the work of a master. Aside from appearance, though, the cathedral had special meaning for the 19-year-old Joan, a devout Catholic since childhood. Biographers Régine Pernoud and Marie-Véronique Clin wrote, "What we can believe is that for her Reims was the home on earth of St. Remi, a saint she had known as a child . . . what mattered to Joan was her assurance of God's presence and action there."[2]

The ritual in the cathedral started at nine in the morning. The archbishop of Reims stood poised to perform the most sacred part of the ceremony. Nobles sent by Charles had ridden their horses to St. Remi abbey, where the holy oil, called Sainte Ampoule, was kept. The four knights accompanied the abbott, who carried the oil, to the city. They entered the cathedral on horseback. The king recited an oath of loyalty, and a benediction was held for the royal insignia, which was made up of a crown, golden spurs, a scepter, and a second scepter carved in ivory.

The archbishop placed a drop of the holy oil on the crown prince's head, shoulders, chest, and wrists as he lay facedown. After he was anointed, Charles stood and put on a tunic and a silk coat. He slipped on gloves, and then the ring that bound him to his people was placed on his finger. Finally, the crown was placed on his head. (Those in charge of the ceremony

A photo of the house where Joan of Arc was born in 1412. Her home village in France, originally named Domrémy, has since been renamed Domrémy-la-Pucelle after Joan's nickname, *la Pucelle d'Orléans* ("the Maid of Orleans").

had to use a different crown, as the traditional one was in the English-controlled city of Paris.) According to tradition, Charles VII, the new king of France, was now divinely blessed by Christ.

Joan, deeply moved, knelt before her king when the ceremony had ended and said, "Gentle king, now the will of God has been accomplished, who wished that I should raise the siege of Orleans and bring you to this city of Reims to receive your solemn consecration, showing that you are the true king, that you are he to whom the kingdom of France should belong."[3]

After the ceremony ended, Charles rode around the city on horseback, with Joan by his side. Though the story conjures up a heroic figure, Charles was the opposite. He was not physically attractive, nor did he exude the power expected of a king. According to author Mary Gordon, "He had small and squinty eyes. He had short legs and was knock-kneed."[4] Author Marina Warner described him as "restless, impatient, devious, and distrustful."[5] He was easily influenced and weak when it came to decision making. "Though aware of his defects and weaknesses," Warner wrote, "Joan believed in the powers of ceremony to change a private into a king."[6]

As she and the new king made their way through the city, people sought to touch the girl who had given them hope that their country might be saved. After the coronation, Joan was set on leading the king and his soldiers to overthrow the English in Paris. She immediately tried to persuade King Charles to move forward, but he, as was his habit, turned to others for their opinions. He began to lean toward negotiating with the English. Weeks passed. Joan had confided to her closest comrades on the march to Reims that she "feared nothing except treason."[7] At the same time, many who supported the English king had grown to fear and despise her. She worried that if King Charles continued to wait, all would be lost. Not only her country's fate, but her own, hung in the balance.

Childhood

Joan of Arc was born either in 1412 or 1413, on or about January 6. Her birth date is not known because few careful records were kept in the Middle Ages, and most were recorded by and for nobles. Joan's father, Jacques d'Arc, and her mother, Isabelle Romee, who attached the name *Romee* to her given name after she made a religious pilgrimage to Rome, were peasants in Domrémy-la-Pucelle, a village that bordered Champagne and Lorraine in northeastern France.

Joan's nickname in her village was Jhenette (little Joan); today in France they refer to her as Jeanne. She never heard herself called Jeanne d'Arc (Joan of Arc), a name first used in 1455, more than two decades after her death. Joan had an older brother who left home when she was still a child; a sister, Catherine, who died young; and two brothers,

Jean and Pierre. Her father had a leading role in the village as a sergeant and was put in charge of collecting taxes. Sometimes travelers boarded at the d'Arc house, which was sizable. They owned approximately 50 acres (20.2 hectares) of land in the village, as well as their house and their furniture, and unlike many other peasants of the era, even had a little money set aside.

No one is exactly sure what Joan looked like. No accurate portraits done in her lifetime exist. Historians have guessed at her height and weight based on armor that is believed to have belonged to Joan. She is believed to have been around 5 feet (152 centimeters) tall. Her build is assumed to be slight, and though often portrayed as fair and tall, she was in fact dark haired and probably had an olive complexion.

Joan was like the other girls in her village, whose mothers taught them household tasks. She learned to spin wool and sew and probably helped tend the sheep. If anything set Joan apart from her peers, it was her natural kindness and her devotion to God. She loved the ringing of the church bells, and many villagers recalled her attending mass at the nearby church often. She was often described by those who knew her as especially pious, or religious.

JOAN'S WORLD

Examining the world in which Joan was raised will help us understand the religious, material, and political influences that shaped her life. During her youth, the kingdom of France was split between the French and the English. The people of France were divided by their loyalty to the nation's two kings. They were also divided by class. There was the peasantry and the nobility, and little in between. Language also divided the nation: Joan grew up speaking French, but German was spoken north and east of her, and Flemish or Dutch in the north.

Some scholars believe this simple drawing of Joan of Arc is the only illustration made of her during her lifetime. Note that Joan is portrayed carrying her standard and sword. The accompanying text mentions the lifting of the siege of Orleans in 1429.

But land—the control of it, the desire by the nobility to conquer more of it—was the major cause of divisions in Joan's France. Her village of Domrémy-la-Pucelle was on the edge of the duchy (land owned by dukes) of Lorraine, but was under the rule of the kingdom of France. The Duke of Lorraine was the king of Germany and Bohemia. He was also the overlord of one large section of Domrémy-la-Pucelle, with the king of France considered the overlord in the d'Arc family's section. Burgundy was south of Lorraine, and the Duke of Burgundy was in control of Flanders (today partly in Belgium and partly in Holland), where both French and Flemish were spoken.

Land was the greatest symbol of wealth and power in the Middle Ages, and it was either acquired through conquest or through gifts from the king or pope. Knights often represented more than one noble or king because they hoped to have land bestowed on them. After a noble was granted land from the king, he gave each of his vassals (the peasants) a portion of land. In turn, the vassals pledged their loyalty and armed service for the many battles that were necessary to keep the land and the income it produced. Creating a family dynasty was another method of claiming land, and marriages were arranged around this concept. The system produced great power and wealth among the aristocracy.

Like most other European nations of the period, France had a social hierarchy with the king at the top. Below the king were dukes, who ruled large provinces, followed by counts, barons, and serfs. It was not uncommon for dukes to be wealthier than the king. The people they protected fought to conquer more land for their lord, the duke. The greatest feudal lord of the era was the pope. Bishops and abbots also sought and acquired land.

Starting in 1348 and continuing into Joan's era and beyond, nearly half the population of France perished from the Black Death (widely thought to have been an outbreak of bubonic plague), famine, poverty, and massacres.[1] Because of the loss of so much manpower, the traditional feudal hierarchy was undergoing great change during Joan's childhood. The noblemen and the church, which had depended on household taxes of the peasantry for their wealth and power, began to fight over land. Serfdom—a condition of bondage like slavery through which nobles controlled peasants—was disappearing. Knights were also decreasing in number, as it was becoming the custom to pay soldiers, instead of simply promising them a portion of conquered land.

THE HUNDRED YEARS' WAR

The ongoing war with England, fought mostly on French soil, took a terrible toll. The war started in 1339 when King Edward III of England learned that King Philip of France had taken over his French holdings. Edward's mother, Isabella, was the daughter of King Philip IV. As Edward saw it, this meant he was the rightful heir to the French throne especially since the current French king had no male heirs. King Edward was determined to recover the territories England had once held in France.

In August 1346, the English waged a mighty battle against the French at a place called Crécy in northern France. The French were certain of victory, as they were known to be great fighters. The English, however, had the advantage because of the development of a new style of combat. Welsh knifemen, pikemen, and trained archers were new additions to the military. The French were confused by the new method of fighting. The Battle of Crécy started a French losing streak in the war. After the English victory at the Battle of Agincourt in 1415, the Treaty of Troyes was signed. The treaty gave the rule of France and England to the future son of Henry V (1387–1422), who had agreed to marry Catherine, the sister of the French king, Charles VII.

It is easy to see how the gloomy atmosphere in France caused insecurity among the French people, especially in the young. By the time Joan was a teenager, people in France were convinced that the English had already won the war.

CIVIL WAR

Adding to the general feeling of hopelessness in France was the fact that the nation was also in the midst of civil war. In 1407, the Duke of Burgundy, known as John the Fearless, assassinated his first cousin, Louis of Orleans, and threw Louis's body into the street. In response, Bernard VII, comte d'Armagnac, started a faction called the Armagnacs. This group set out to avenge the death of Louis. Twelve years later, the dauphin, Charles VII, asked for a meeting with John the Fearless, with the intention of restoring peace between Burgundy and the royal family. John agreed, and as they were in discussion on a bridge, someone with an ax ran up and killed John in front of the dauphin. The mystery of who planned the assassination was never solved. The English saw the perfect opportunity to step in and enlist the aid of the Burgundians in their quest to control all of France. John's successor, Philip the Good, entered a joint war with the English against Charles VI, father of the crown prince, who was considered insane. (Today he is thought to have suffered from schizophrenia.)

Joan's village of Domrémy-la-Pucelle was not exempt from all the violence. One of the worst side effects of the wars was the bands of dangerous mercenaries who roamed the countryside, demanding money from people for protection and taking whatever they wanted. When Joan was 16, the Burgundy governor of Champagne led an unsuccessful attack, in which buildings in Domrémy-la-Pucelle were burned, including the St. Remi church. In the chaos, Joan and her family went to the nearby town of Neufchâteau seeking protection. While they were waiting to return to their village, Joan was accused of breaking a promise of marriage. Joan claimed she had not done this, defended herself in court, and won.

An oil-on-panel portrait of John the Fearless (also known as also John II, Duke of Burgundy, and John of Valois), whose actions helped spark a civil war in France.

RELIGION'S IMPACT

The Roman Catholic Church also contributed to the chaos of the era. The Church of France was part of the greater Catholic Church. The spiritual leader was the pope in Rome, and the French church was led by a conference of French bishops. From the time the first French king, Clovis I, was crowned, Catholicism had been the official state religion. Since that time, the king of France was referred to as His Most Christian Majesty; this happened almost 1,000 years before Joan's birth. In 800, Charlemagne was crowned emperor of the Holy Roman Empire by Pope Leo III, which set the foundation for a Christian French empire.

Then political differences and theological disputes began to divide the Catholic Church. The so-called Great Schism of 1054 caused a split between the Eastern and Western Christian churches. In 1378, a second division, the Great Western Schism, further fragmented the church. At the time of Joan's birth, three men were claiming to be pope of the Roman Catholic Church. They were located in Rome, in Avignon, France, and in Spain. Wars being fought in Italy caused the pope in Rome to move to Avignon. France and England were at war, and the rulers in England, along with authorities of its allies Germany and Italy, were unhappy about the pope's move to France. They knew this meant that money and power would flood into France. The allies put pressure on the church to return the pope to Rome. When an election for a new pope was held, the papacy returned to Rome in 1378, and Romans demanded that an Italian be elected. The church leaders elected Urban VI. They then learned of his violent temper and claimed that he should not be pope. The French cardinals that voted for Urban VI blamed their hasty decision on the threatening crowd that had gathered at the time of the election. The French cardinals tried to rectify the situation and elected a new pope, claiming that Urban VI's election was invalid.

War in Spain also inspired several other figures to claim the papacy. Clement VII, a Frenchman, was officially elected, but Urban would not step down. The Great Western Schism was finally ended at the Council of Constance (1414–1418), but much doubt remained as to which pope was the true authority. Both Urban VI and Clement VII were finally deposed in favor of Martin V.

The church had been corrupt under the two former popes, whose greed led to the rise of men who demanded reform in the church. One of them, Jan Hus, a Czech priest, became popular. Hus believed the Bible should be translated from Latin into a language everyone could read. For this and other then-radical beliefs, Hus was burned as a heretic in 1416. Church officials were threatened by the new popular movement, which was anti-authoritarian. Such movements stressed "private inspiration and the primacy of the individual conscience,"[2] the exact opposite of what the church then preached. In response, the church stepped up its authoritarian rule. It also aligned itself with the country they predicted to win the Hundred Years' War—England.

HEARING VOICES

The citizens of Joan's village were barely affected by the shifts occurring within the administration of the Roman Church. They were good Catholics who believed in the Eucharist (the bread and wine consumed during Holy Communion), prayer, and frequent confessions. They had "a love and respect for others, a willingness to welcome and help strangers, and a joyously active daily life."[3] They also practiced folk traditions that had been handed down from pagan (pre-Christian) times. Joan, for example, joined other girls in dancing around what was known as a fairy tree. Sometimes the girls hung garlands on the tree. All of these traditional rituals were considered perfectly normal.

Peasants could not read or write, and Joan was no exception. News of war victories and defeats arrived via word of mouth. Legends and prophecies were handed down and were quite popular. One prophecy that held a special fascination among all classes in France, including the king and the Catholic clerics, claimed that a maid would come from the ancient wood to save France. Of this prophecy, Christine de Pisan, a poet and historian who died in 1430, wrote:

> It was found in the history records that she [Joan] was destined to accomplish her mission; for more than 500 years ago, Merlin [the wizard in the legends of King Arthur], the Sibyl and Bede foresaw her coming, entered her in their writings as someone who would put an end to France's troubles, made prophecies about her, saying that she would carry the banner in the French wars.[4]

A prophet named Marie d'Avignon also spoke of a maid who would deliver the kingdom of France from its enemies. Since prophecy and mysticism were quite common as Joan entered her teens, she was very aware of various women mystics such as Catherine of Siena, who spoke of receiving visions and hearing voices before her death in 1380. St. Colette of Corbie was another. This was, according to Mary Gordon, "one of the few ways by which medieval women could speak with public authority, certain of being listened to."[5]

In the summer of 1424, when she was around 12 years old, Joan began hearing voices. She was playing with friends when she was told by one of the voices to hurry home to help her mother. Her mother said she had not sent for her. According to a letter written to the Duke of Milan, when Joan returned to her friends, "a shining cloud came down before her eyes, and a voice speaking of the cloud told her: 'Joan, you must lead another life and perform wondrous deeds; for you are she whom the King of Heaven has chosen to bring reparation to the kingdom of France and help and protection to King Charles."[6] Initially frightened by the voices, Joan was left "stupefied by so many marvels."[7]

TWO MARTYRS AND AN ARCHANGEL

When she first heard voices, Joan thought that it was God speaking to her. Later, when she was imprisoned and was being tried as a heretic, she gave the voices the names of saints she had known as a child: St. Catherine, St. Margaret, and St. Michael.

According to Mary Gordon, author of *Joan of Arc*, "Female saints have an especially important function for young girls, since they provide examples of heroism outside the sphere of the domestic; the simplest girl has access to models who defied authority and made a place for themselves in the larger world."*

The two saints Joan named were virgin martyrs who had died in order to remain pure. St. Catherine of Alexandria lived circa 310 A.D. She was born to a wealthy family and had been converted to Christianity by a vision of Our Lady and the Holy Child. The Roman emperor, Maximinus, persecuted Christians, and offered to marry Catherine if she would deny her faith. She refused, saying that she would remain a virgin bride of Christ. Maximinus appointed 50 philosophers to convince Catherine to marry him, but they were won over by her. Maximinus had the philosophers burned to death. He then sentenced Catherine to death. She was to be killed on a spiked wheel, but the wheel broke. Ultimately, he had her beheaded. After her death, she was recognized as a saint.

St. Margaret of Antioch's father had driven her out of her home when she became a Christian. A prefect named Olybrius

Joan later testified that it was summer, around noon, when she heard a voice that seemed to come from the church next door. It was accompanied by a "great light."[8] The third time she heard a voice, she knew it was an

tried to seduce her. When she refused him, he had her tortured and imprisoned. Executioners tried to kill her by fire and by drowning, but she lived. Thousands of spectators who witnessed this miracle were killed before she was beheaded.

An archangel of God, St. Michael, or "Miycha'el" (meaning "who is like God" in Hebrew), appears in both the Old Testament and the New Testament. He defeated Lucifer and the fallen angels in the war in Heaven described in the Book of Revelation. St. Michael, a symbol of national resistance in France during the Hundred Years' War, was named the patron saint of the royal army of France and patron of the island of Mont Saint-Michel. The island was one of few places north of the Loire River that "remained loyal to the French dauphin despite repeated attempts to take it by storm."** St. Michael had great significance for France's future. According to historian Timothy Wilson-Smith: "After Charles VII's son became king, he created the order of St. Michael, and that island [Mont Saint-Michel] was the center of his new order of chivalry."***

*Mary Gordon, *Joan of Arc*. New York: The Penquin Group, 2000, p. 23.
**Timothy Wilson-Smith, *Joan of Arc: Maid, Myth and History*. London: The History Press, p. 11.
***Ibid.

angel's. (When pressured later in her life to say to whom the voices belonged, she claimed that the voices were those of St. Catherine, St. Margaret, and St. Michael.) The voices were specific in their commands. She was to find the king, defeat the English at Orleans, and ensure that he was crowned at Reims. Once this was accomplished, she was to rescue the Duke of Orleans from imprisonment in England and restore Paris to French rule.

FOLLOWING HER VOICES

Joan did not want to worry her parents, so she decided not to tell them about the voices. Her father had a dream that may have caused her to hesitate. According to her mother, he dreamed that Joan was a camp follower with an army, and he told her brothers that if anything like that occurred, he would direct them to drown her.

Later, Joan went to the home of her cousin by marriage, Durand Laxart, where she stayed for a week. She convinced Laxart that he should take her to Vaucouleurs, a few miles away, and introduce her to the captain of the town. After she explained her mission, Laxart felt compelled to help her. When asked about his role years later, he said, "Was it not said that France would be ruined through a woman, and afterwards restored by a Virgin?"[9] (The woman he believed had destroyed France was the mother of the dauphin, Queen Isabella of Bavaria, and the woman who would save France was Joan of Arc.)

Meeting the Future King

Once he agreed to help Joan, Durand Laxart told Joan's father that she should stay and help his wife, who was then pregnant. In May 1428, Laxart and Joan traveled to Vaucouleurs, where Robert de Baudricourt was captain of the town. Joan wore a man's red coat over her dress. De Baudricourt, known for his womanizing and looting, probably agreed to meet with her out of curiosity. He was not prepared for the feisty Joan, who approached him as an equal and wasted no time in telling him that she had come in the name of the Lord. The crown prince, Charles VII, she announced, must meet with her. Annoyed, de Baudricourt ordered Laxart to return Joan to her father's house.

Undaunted, Joan returned to de Baudricourt a second time in January 1429 and implored him once more to take her to the dauphin. Again he turned her away. What de Baudricourt did not yet know was that some of his soldiers had started to pledge loyalty to the maiden who kept declaring she was there to save their country. They found her presence and her words inspiring.

Two men, Jean de Metz and Bertrand de Poulengy, were especially drawn to her and her mission. De Metz later wrote about his experience and recalled Joan's reply to de Baudricourt when he refused to believe her: "'I must be at the king's side,' she said, 'though I wear my feet to the knees. For indeed there is nobody in all the world, neither king nor duke, nor daughter of the King of Scotland, nor any other who can recover the kingdom of France.'"[1] De Metz, though approximately 57 years old at the time, became Joan's servant: "I had a great trust in what the maid said, and I was on fire with what she said and with a love for her which was, as I believe, a divine love. I believe that she was sent by God."[2]

At this time, Joan started introducing herself as Jeanne La Pucelle, or Joan the Maid. *Pucelle* means "virgin," but in Old French it meant "a young girl," and refers to innocence and youth and desirability. Warner wrote that "she picked a word for virginity that captured with double strength the magic of her state in her culture. It expressed not only the incorruption of her body, but also the dangerous border into maturity or full womanhood that she had not crossed and would not cross."[3]

OFF TO SEE THE KING

As Joan waited for de Baudricourt to make up his mind about whether or not to support her, an old duke, Charles of Lorraine, summoned her. He was ill and wanted the maid to heal him. The duke had left his wife for another woman years before. Together they had five children. Joan boldly told him that he should return to his wife. To everyone's surprise, he humbly accepted her advice. He gave her a black horse and four francs. Then Joan made a deal with him. In return for the help of the duke's son, the Duke of Anjou, Joan would pray for Charles's recovery. Charles agreed to the terms.

When she returned from visiting the duke, Joan dressed in her uncle's clothes and went to find the dauphin on her own. But after stopping to pray, she returned to Vaucouleurs. The voices had clearly said that de Baudricourt should lead her. On the way back to Vaucouleurs, the voices told Joan that the English had overtaken Orleans, a beautiful port city situated on the Loire River. When Joan met with de Baudricourt again, she told him about the English conquest of Orleans. He agreed to persuade the king to meet with her.

Joan began to prepare for the meeting. When de Metz asked her about her clothing, she said she preferred men's attire. The citizens of the town provided men's clothes and gave her a horse. Accompanied by the Duke of Anjou, the knights who had decided to follow her, and soldiers provided by de Baudricourt, on February 23, 1429, Joan started the 350-mile (563-kilometer) journey to Chinon, where she was to meet Charles VII. Surprisingly, the party encountered no major setbacks or obstacles on their journey. As biographer Mary Gordon described it: "It's as if Dorothy got to Oz with no interference from the wicked witch. As if a girl from the boondocks decided to see the president and made her way to the Oval Office without passing through metal detectors."[4]

The travelers arrived in Chinon on March 6. Though Charles VII had agreed to an interview with Joan, he was not convinced that she had anything special to offer. Some of his councilors were strongly opposed to helping her, including Charles's chamberlain (the officer in charge of managing the household of a nobleman), Georges de La Tremoille. The fabulously wealthy, unusually tall, obese

An oil-on-panel portrait of King Charles VII of France, by Jean Fouquet. In 1429, Charles was crowned in Reims with the aid of Joan of Arc in order to free France from the English.

chamberlain had tremendous influence over the 26-year-old dauphin.

Charles was "cunning, timid and superstitious"[5] and easily swayed by others. The only surviving child of five boys, he had an aura of sadness around him. "The most famous surviving portrait of Charles, by Jean Fouquet, shows a man with sorrowful eyes starting bleakly from either side of a bulbous nose, a picture of world-weariness."[6] Charles's political position was precarious, as the English were winning the Hundred Years' War and France did not have enough money or men to overtake them. He also carried doubts about his legitimacy, as his mother claimed he was the result of an affair. Charles was indecisive and often procrastinated. He relied heavily on the advice of others to make any decision.

La Tremoille saw the young maiden who came to crown her king as a threat to his own authority with the dauphin. And their advice to the dauphin could not have been more different: La Tremoille's policy was to negotiate with the enemy rather than engage in battle. Joan was the opposite. "She despised truces and felt that the Burgundians could only be spoken to 'at the end of a lance.'"[7]

Charles decided to test Joan. He dressed as a commoner and stood with the hundreds of courtiers who had gathered while someone else pretended to be king. Joan entered with great fanfare and made her way directly to Charles. She fell to her knees and said, "Very noble Lord dauphin, I am come and sent by God to bring succor to you and your kingdom."[8]

The dauphin was impressed by this and asked Joan to speak with him in private. No one overheard their conversation, and the words that were exchanged have never been revealed. What is known is that Charles appeared changed afterward. Normally depressed and lethargic, he was now enthusiastic. Joan, as a symbolic act, had Charles turn over his kingdom to her, whereupon she put it in the hands of God, who had directed her to "invest King Charles with the kingdom of France."[9] According to Gordon, "She has power over Charles, but it comes from God, and it is God moving through her who will enable the actions that must, if they are going to be effectual in this world, come from the king."[10]

The moment Joan of Arc recognizes the disguised dauphin, later King Charles VII of France, at Chinon in 1429 is captured in this nineteenth-century wood engraving.

TESTS

In spite of Charles's confidence in Joan, he and the members of his council did not rush to provide an army. They instructed her to go to Poitiers so the learned clergymen at the university there could examine her. Charles needed more proof that she was divinely inspired, and he also sought the church's approval. For 11 days, Joan answered their questions with boldness, intelligence, and little tweaks of humor. One question they asked was why, if it were God's will that she drive the English back to England, did she need soldiers? Her response was curt. She said that "the soldiers were to fight in God's name and that God would give the victory."[11] By the end of the interview, the clergymen were convinced that Joan was indeed the virgin who had come to save France. Only a few written lines were ever uncovered from the trial at Poitiers, but one conclusion is known: "That in her is found no evil, but only good, humility, virginity, devotion, honesty, simplicity."[12]

Joan left Poitiers on March 25, which was Good Friday and the feast of the Annunciation, which celebrated the angel Gabriel's announcement to Mary that she would become the mother of the Son of God. She set out on a pilgrimage to Notre-Dame cathedral at Le Puy-en-Velay. She was accompanied by six of her men, her mother, and Jean Pasquerel, the lector at a nearby convent. Pasquerel became Joan's confessor and traveled with her everywhere.

The next step was for Joan to go to Tours, where it would be confirmed that she was a virgin. This was an important issue, as virginity was considered "the sign of one who dedicates himself or herself wholly to God."[13] By calling herself Jeanne La Pucelle, or Joan the Maid, she was declaring her virginity. "The test of virginity was above all a proof of sincerity."[14]

Based on the positive reports from Poitiers and Tours, Charles sent Joan to Orleans to fight the English. He agreed to provide everything she needed. She was fitted for armor in Tours—a bassinet, or helmet, body armor, and leg and arm harnesses. The helmet made for her had a small, moveable visor and also protected her neck. A steel hat with a wide brim, called a capeline, was useful when scaling walls and being bombarded with stones. (Joan preferred riding with her head bare.) The body armor was made of steel plates. The vest portion was called a brigandine. One man who saw her said that she appeared "armed entirely in

JOAN THE MAID

Joan of Arc's virginity had great significance to the people of France. Contained within the prophecy that France would be saved by a woman, it was stressed that she would be a virgin savior. "Chastity was the touchstone of female virtue; it was widely believed that the devil could not have commerce with a virgin."*

Joan was tested several times for proof of her virginity, though there was then little scientific knowledge about the female body. If she had been found not to be a virgin, she would have been sent home, for it would have made her a liar. "In Joan's time, those men and women who consecrated themselves to God showed their acceptance of the divine call by remaining virgin . . . totally at the Lord's service in heart and body."**

In fact, since the second century, Christians believed that "the body of a woman was one of the holiest things possible in creation, holier than the chastity of a man."***

Jean d'Aulon, her good friend and companion, when testifying in her behalf a year later, said that "although he had seen white, except for the head, a little ax in her hand, seated on a great black courser."[15]

Robert de Baudricourt gave her a sword, but Joan asked her men to retrieve another, which was hidden behind the altar of the Sainte-Catherine de Fierbois church. When the men found it and asked how she knew it was there, she said that her voices had told her its location. She then asked Scottish painter Hauves Poulnoir to design a standard and a small pennon, which was a long, narrow flag often attached

her naked body, he had never felt any sexual desire for her."****
He was not alone. There are many testimonies of brave young men who experienced such reverence for her.

According to the men who were closest to her, Joan did not menstruate. It was mentioned often that Joan ate and drank little, which may have been the cause. (This is a common side effect of anorexia today, and women athletes, including dancers, sometimes do not menstruate.) Whatever the cause, it added to the purity and holiness that has been attributed to her.

---

*Marina Warner, *Joan of Arc: The Image of Female Heroism*, p. 14.
**Regine Pernoud and Marie-Veronique Clin, *Joan of Arc: Her Story*, p. 31.
***Marina Warner, *Joan of Arc: The Image of Female Heroism*, p. 24.
****Timothy Wilson-Smith, *Joan of Arc: Maid, Myth and History*, p. 107.

to the lances of medieval knights. The scene depicted on her pennon was of the archangel Gabriel presenting the Virgin Mary with a double lily.

The fleur-de-lis traditionally represented French royalty. Tradition holds that Clovis, the first French king, received a golden lily from an angel upon his conversion to Christianity. A symbol of his purification, it later came to symbolize perfection and light. Another legend said that Clovis adopted the symbol when water lilies helped him cross a river. In the twelfth century, either King Louis VI or King Louis VII was the first French king to put the fleur-de-lis on his shield. From that time forward, it was used as the royal insignia. These banners were to have a huge symbolic effect on her soldiers as Joan led them into war in the name of God.

Jean d'Aulon served as Joan's master of household, and Etienne de Vignolles, called "La Hire," which means anger, was a ferocious soldier who was devoted to her. Joan was treated as a warrior of high rank. She had pages and heralds who delivered messages and five warhorses. Her brothers, Pierre and Jean, joined her. They set off with horsemen, men-at-arms, cattle, wagons, priests—and 4,000 men—to Orleans to attack the British.

On April 21, 1429, they headed to a town called Blois. Joan told the men that she did not want to hear foul language and expected them to take communion regularly. Even the mercenary soldier La Hire went to confession and did not use vulgar terms in front of Joan. They were all willing to oblige, for in their eyes she had offered them the "hope of divine assistance."[16]

The Journey
to Reims

Eighty miles (129 km) south of Paris, the city of Orleans then had a population of 30,000. If the English were to move further south into France, the English needed to conquer Orleans. The Duke of Bedford, the regent of England, planned the attack, assisted by Duke Philip the Good of Burgundy, as Orleans was difficult to penetrate. It had been attacked so many times that the citizens had built strong fortifications around it. Five gates offered entry into the city: the Burgundy Gate, the Paris Gate, the Bernier Gate, the Renard Gate, and the St. Catherine Gate. "Each gate was flanked by two towers protected by a heavy grating, called a portcullis, that could be lowered and raised. Earthen embankments were the first line of defense."[1]

Towers situated on either side of every gate protected the bridges into the city. To further protect themselves, the citizens of Orleans had blocked three of the gates, leaving only the Burgundy and St. Catherine gates open.

In October 1428, the English had begun a siege of the city. Their goal was to make the inhabitants prisoners in their own city. Food and other supplies could not be brought in. The method the English used to isolate the city was to set up *bastides*, or temporary fortifications, outside each gate of the city. These could be small structures that sometimes housed troops whose job was to ensure nothing entered the city. There was continuous fighting over the next months, and by March 1429 the city was ready to fall to the English. After capturing Orleans, the plan was to attack the dauphin at Bourges, in the center of France.

Twenty-five-year-old John, the Count of Dunois, Bastard of Orleans, was acting as lieutenant governor when the attacks started. His younger half brother, Charles, the Duke of Orleans, would normally have been in charge. But Charles had been a prisoner in England since October 25, 1415, when he was wounded and captured during the Battle of Agincourt. Another of Joan's goals was to bring Charles back to France.

The standard set by the code of chivalry was that a city could not be besieged if the lord of that city was being held prisoner. Dunois suggested to the Duke of Bedford that if the English would refrain from attacking Orleans, the city would remain neutral in the war. The Duke of Bedford would have none of it. He replied, "I would be mighty angry to cut down the bushes so that someone else could get the little birds from the branches!"[2] The negotiations broke down.

Dunois, who was suffering from a wounded foot, worried that his city would end up like the besieged city of Rouen. In 1417, its starving citizens had been forced to eat dogs and rats before they surrendered their city to the

In this illustration of Joan of Arc in armor and riding horse, William Blake Richmond portrays her as an inspirational military leader and French heroine.

English. The situation could not have been worse. Dunois began to hear rumors of the maiden sent by God to save France. He sent two trusted men to Chinon to see if there was any truth to it. They returned and reported they had seen a maid moving about Chinon as she waited to be granted an audience with the king. They told him that she demanded horses, men, and arms in order to "raise the siege of Orleans and to lead the noble dauphin to Reims, so that he could be anointed king."[3]

ARRIVAL OF JOAN

Joan and her soldiers, followed by a caravan of supply wagons, left Blois and traveled toward Orleans along the south bank of the Loire. The English were on the north bank. Joan realized only after bypassing Orleans that Dunois wanted supplies more than he wanted Joan of Arc to save his city. The sight of Joan and her army approaching must have been a shock to him. A biography of Joan written in the early 1500s states:

> The Maid, arrayed in white armour, rode on horseback before the King, with her standard unfurled. When not in armour, she kept state as a knight and dressed as one. Her shoes were tied with laces to her feet, her horse and doublet were shapely, a hat was on her head. She wore very handsome attire of cloth of gold and silk, noticeably trimmed with fur.[4]

Dunois rode out to meet Joan, who wasted no time in demanding whether it was he who had caused the detour. In a condescending voice, he told her that he and other wise men had decided it was the safer way. Joan said, "I bring you better help than ever came to you from any soldier to any city, as it is the help of the King of Heaven. It comes not from me but from God Himself."[5]

Unconvinced that she was any kind of savior, Dunois turned from her to focus on bigger worries. The supplies Orleans so desperately needed had been loaded onto boats that had to sail against the current. The fierce winds, however, would prevent the voyage to his city. It was at that moment that he witnessed what he believed was a miracle, which, coupled with the fact that the English were ignoring them, changed his mind about Joan. She stood calmly in the gale force winds, which suddenly died down and allowed the supplies to reach their destination.

On April 29, 1429, Joan entered Orleans carrying her banner. Her two brothers rode with her. She was followed by lords, squires, and men-at-arms. People of Orleans emerged to catch a glimpse of Joan, overjoyed at the prospect of being rescued, and reached out to touch this teenage girl and her horse as they rode by. On April 30, Joan presented herself to Dunois, only to learn that he would not fight until he received reinforcements from the king. She walked out to view the enemy, some within hearing distance. She yelled at them to "go away in God's name, otherwise she would drive them out."[6] They hurled insults back at her. She marched up to a rampart and told the English to surrender. They shouted back at her that "they would burn her if they ever got hold of her."[7]

Joan stuck to the chivalric code of not fighting on a Sunday, but it was getting harder to abide by such codes because the enemy was not interested in following rules. On May 4, after French reinforcements arrived, Dunois and Joan dined together. He told her he had learned that the English were sending a new army to Orleans, led by John Fastolf, an accomplished soldier. Joan saw an even greater challenge than she had imagined, and welcomed it. She knew she would have to gain ground quickly in order to encourage the French and gain their support. Her voices awoke her in the middle of the night, and she decided to act. There had been a skirmish near the Burgundy Gate. When Joan got there, the English were preparing for an active defense. When Joan appeared, the French fought harder and soon had taken the bastide and fortress.

In this oil-on-canvas painting by Jean-Jacques Scherrer, the triumphant entrance of Joan of Arc into Orleans in 1429 is depicted.

Joan was distressed by the deaths that resulted from this battle, both English and French. She immediately went to confession, asking her soldiers to do the same and to thank

God for their victory. She also prayed for the dead. She decided not to fight the next day, the Feast of the Ascension, which is the Christian holiday that commemorates the day Jesus Christ ascended into heaven in the presence of his apostles after his resurrection. Instead, she dictated three letters to the English, filled with orders for them to leave or be prepared to take the consequences. The English kidnapped her messenger, so she tied her next letter to an arrow and commanded an archer to shoot it across enemy lines. The English shouted insults at her.

Joan and Dunois disagreed on the next course of action. He wanted to wait. She went ahead with her men to a bastide, which they found deserted. She assumed the English had moved to a stronger fortress. Joan and La Hire led the way in a sneak attack against the English, overtaking the bastide. Most of the English were killed. To Joan's amazement, the French captains of the city decided to delay any further attacks because the English outnumbered them. Joan, however, was a girl of action. Preparing for battle, she told her chaplain and confessor, Jean Pasquerel, to stay close to her when they attacked, for she knew she would be wounded. The following day, Joan and her men attacked the fortress of Tourelles, and, as she had predicted, an arrow hit her above her breast. It was a shallow wound that was treated with olive oil and bacon fat, after which she raced back into battle.

Under Joan's command, her men filled a barge with tar and sticks, set it on fire, and sent it under the fortress bridge. Dunois wanted the army to return to the walls of the city, but Joan ordered them to stop and take some food and drink, hoping that nourishment would give them a second wind. She handed her standard to a squire, whom Jean d'Aulon told to follow Joan and himself to a ditch. Joan did not hear his order, and when she saw the squire in the ditch, she grabbed her banner, which started to wave back and forth. Her men thought it was a signal to attack and rushed to follow her command. They took the bastide, which the English had abandoned during the assault.

On Sunday, May 8, the English exited their bastides and stood in battle formation. Joan did the same with her army. For an hour, the enemies stood facing each other. The French, flush with their recent victory, were itching to fight again. The English, however, "raised and totally abandoned the siege that they had laid to Orleans from the twelfth day of October 1428 up to this day."[8] They left behind food supplies and weapons. Orleans was liberated. There was a great celebration that night.

Joan went to see the dauphin, who was thrilled with her achievements. He was not alone. Her victory at Orleans had a huge impact on all French citizens. "The French . . . had risen and countered the greatest military effort of their conquerors by throwing them into the Loire—and this feat was credited to a young girl of sixteen or seventeen. She was an inspired virgin from whom one could expect almost any miracle."[9]

A SPECIAL FRIEND

Joan was already thinking about what she would need to do to fulfill the next order from her voices: The dauphin needed to be crowned king. Charles's advisers wanted him to march to Normandy, but Joan was insistent that they go to Reims for his coronation, which would make Charles the legitimate king in the eyes of his people. Joan had a deep understanding of symbolism and its power. As she herself was a symbol, she knew that Charles, once crowned, would be seen as the rightful heir and a figure for the French to rally around.

Joan went to meet with John, the Duke of Alencon, who had been freed after paying a huge ransom to his British captor, the Duke of Clarence. To John's great relief, now that the Battle of Orleans had been a success, he would not have to surrender two important territories to the English

This stone plaque in Basilique Saint-Denis, France, shows the type of armor worn by Joan of Arc. What Joan wore would later become a source of controversy at her trial.

Duke of Bedford. A member of the royal council, John had been taken prisoner at Verneuil on August 6, 1424. His wife had pawned her jewelry in order to free him, but it took five years to settle the score with his captors. Ransom was a common way to acquire money and land in the Middle Ages when important men were captured in battle. It was far more profitable than killing such wealthy prisoners, but it could take years for the ransom amount to be agreed upon, and then for it to be paid.

KNIGHTS

Biographer Marina Warner wrote, "The sacredness of the bond between a knight and a lord cannot be overstressed."* Charles VII honored Joan by making her a knight. Joan's village of Domrémy-la-Pucelle held dear the ideals of knighthood, and it is certain that Joan grew up hearing tales of knights.

Knights were held in the highest esteem during the Middle Ages because they were considered Christian soldiers who adhered to the code of chivalry. Knights considered self-sacrifice, generosity, and personal honor to be of the utmost importance. According to Warner, "Leaders should be bold and rash, careless of their lives, eager to lay themselves down for their followers . . . a kind of bravura, of foolhardy recklessness was prized as the badge of great courage."** Knights also loved rich clothing, and Joan of Arc was no exception. According to Warner, "The imprisoned Duke of Orleans, Charles, ordered a splendid costume for her [Joan] as a token of his gratitude after the raising of the siege."*** Ironically,

Joan and John had met in Chinon, when Joan had visited the king. She had been curious and asked Charles about him. She discovered that he was the godfather to Charles's son, the future Louis XI, and a close friend. Joan replied that "the more the blood of France is gathered together, the better it shall be."[10] From then on she referred to John as "my fair Duke"[11] and he became devoted to her. She met his mother and his wife. When his wife expressed concern about her husband going to battle,

Joan was later severely criticized for making a statement with her clothes.

But, as Mary Gordon asks, was Joan "ever really a knight? She refused ennoblement for herself, asking for it only for her brothers."**** Joan's way of doing things was much simpler. Her speech was direct, her gifts were not grandiose, and she did not like ceremonies. She focused instead on battles and meeting her military goals.

Even as Joan of Arc was bravely leading her soldiers to Paris, the chivalrous ways of the knight were waning, soon to be replaced by paid soldiers who used guns instead of swords.

*Marina Warner, *Joan of Arc: The Image of Female Heroism*, p. 174.
**Ibid., p. 178.
***Ibid., p. 170.
****Mary Gordon, *Joan of Arc*, p. 80.

Joan promised to send him back "in better shape than he is now!"[12]

ON TO REIMS AND THE CORONATION

Joan was prepared to fight the English all the way to Reims if need be. The dauphin put the Duke of Alencon in charge of the Loire campaign. He was given 2,000 men, a number that doubled the next day when Dunois and another captain brought their troops. Still, the captains worried about being outnumbered by the English troops in Jargeau, who were still under the command of John Fastolf.

The English drove back the French soldiers. The Duke of Alencon recalled later: "Seeing this, Joan seized her standard, rode into the fray and found the soldiers displaying great courage."[13] As night approached, the French retired with hope that they would win the next day. Joan attacked early in the morning, and her men took the Earl of Suffolk prisoner. Although Joan was hit by a falling stone as she scaled a ladder, she was spared serious injury because she was wearing a helmet. She then saved the Duke of Alencon's life by warning him to step away from a certain area. (After he moved, a machine fell onto that same spot, killing someone else.) The French were victorious.

Joan moved her men on to Meung and then Beaugency, which they captured quickly, driving the English into the castle. But then she learned that English reinforcements, under the command of Lord Talbot, were on their way. On June 17, 1429, the two armies were in sight of each other. The English called the French to fight, but Joan told them to wait until the next morning. She assured her men that they would defeat the English. Her prophecy proved correct. During the Battle of Patay, which some historians consider to be as important as the Battle of Orleans, the English fled, but not before 4,000 of them were either captured or killed. The English commander was taken, along with about 200 other noblemen who could bring in big ransoms. Since their defeat at the hands of the British during the Battle of Agincourt, the French had suffered many setbacks. But the Battle of Patay was theirs.

The news of the English defeat caused the Burgundians in Paris, who were loyal to the English, to panic. They began to further fortify their city. Joan would have had an advantage if she had been able to move her army quickly to Paris. Approximately 12,000 soldiers were gathered at Gien waiting for Joan. And they had to be paid, which made any delay costly. But the king, following the advice of La Tremoille, chose to continue negotiation with the Burgundians.

Joan could barely control her impatience. She had to wait until June 29 before marching to Reims through lands under Burgundian control. To their surprise, when they entered Auxerre, a delegation came to announce the town's loyalty to the king, as well as the loyalty of the towns of Troyes, Chalons-sur-Marne, and Reims. However, Troyes, where Charles VII had been disinherited, did not declare loyalty until Joan arrived with her soldiers. The townspeople, worried about an assault, surrendered on July 10, and from there Joan and her army headed to Chalons-sur-Marne. The bishop presented the king with the keys of the city. By the time they arrived in Reims, a long column of followers was behind them, hoping to witness the coronation.

The city of Reims offered the king complete obedience. Most of those who had collaborated with the English quickly left town. Charles was anointed and crowned on July 17, 1429. His friend the Duke of Alencon crowned him, and he in turn knighted the duke. Joan's family was there to witness the grand spectacle.

LETDOWN

Pierre Cauchon, a Reims native and former rector of the University of Paris, was among those who left. Though French, he was a strong supporter of the English. A self-made man, he liked all the pomp and splendor associated with the court of Burgundy and had little tolerance for the old French aristocracy. He had become wealthy aiding the Duke of Bedford of England and had been made bishop of Beauvais as a gift from the Burgundian duke, Philip the Good. The crowning of Charles VII at Reims struck horror into his heart and focused his attention on the young woman who was transforming France.

Joan dictated a letter to the Duke of Burgundy on the day of the coronation, which read in part:

> [T]he Maid calls upon you by the King of Heaven, my rightful and sovereign Lord, to make a firm and lasting peace with the king of France. You two must pardon one another fully with a sincere heart, as loyal Christians should; and if it pleases you to make war, go and wage it on the Saracens. Prince of Burgundy, I pray you, supplicate, and humbly request rather than require you, make war no more on the holy kingdom of France . . . As for the gentle king of France, he is ready to make peace with you, saving his honor, if it has to do with you alone.[14]

Joan was not aware that Charles VII's council members were still negotiating with the English and the Burgundians. She had continued to operate under the medieval code of chivalry—either surrender or do battle to the end. As Joan made plans for entering Paris, there were five men who later recalled a remark she made as they were on their way to Reims. Those words would come to haunt her.

Capture at Compiègne

The English had taken Paris in 1417. The Duke of Burgundy and his men had entered the gates of the city, took the king prisoner, and killed as many Armagnacs (the faction that opposed the English and Burgundians) as they could find. The dauphin Charles, who was then 15, was then taken from his bed by an Armagnac captain and moved to central France.

Paris had been under English control ever since, and remained the cultural and political center of France. It had the biggest population north of the Alps. The Parliament of Paris supported the Treaty of Troyes, which had disinherited the dauphin. The University of Paris, whose faculty and clerics were pro-English, was the oldest established university in the kingdom. (The clerics loyal to the French crown had fled to the University of Poitiers.)

The English and Burgundians were stunned by Joan's successes throughout 1429. Though she was revered by the French, she was despised and feared by her enemies. The clergy loyal to the English and Burgundians considered her an enemy of the faith. The English were especially anxious after learning that the region of Champagne had fallen to her and the land south of the Loire was also under Charles VII's control. Though Paris was already strongly fortified, those in charge went to great lengths to make sure Joan could not break through the walls protecting the city. They also did all they could to convince the people of the city to support the Anglo-Burgundian cause. They believed that Henry was the true king of France. Many Parisians had adopted a wait-and-see attitude.

After receiving Joan's plea for harmony on the day of the coronation, July 17, 1429, Philip, the Duke of Burgundy, offered a 15-day truce. He promised that after that time he would offer up Paris to Charles. Joan was suspicious, and rightfully so, for the time wasted by the coronation and negotiations had allowed the Duke of Bedford to make the city more secure. Joan dictated a letter to the citizens of Reims about the truce: "I am not content with the truce . . . and do not know if I will keep it. But if I do keep it, it will be only for the sake of the king's honor."[1]

Joan wanted to attack Paris directly, as it would be impossible to conduct a siege against such a large city. However, Charles's adviser, Georges de La Tremoille, insisted on using diplomacy instead. Some of his reasoning was sound, as the king was worried about how to finance his army; also, they were quite certain that the English and Burgundians outnumbered them. Behind the scenes, however, there was a conflict of interest—La Tremoille's brother was at the Burgundian court, so the king's adviser favored a Franco-Burgundian truce. The more the king and La Tremoille held back, the more impatient Joan became.

In this nineteenth-century illustration, Joan of Arc leads the French army against the English defenders of the Les Tourelles gate during the siege of Orleans on May 7, 1429. Victories such as this one stunned her enemies.

Her fierce independence was becoming a problem for Charles and La Tremoille.

CROSS PURPOSES

The king finally gave Joan permission to march to Soissons. She arrived on July 23. When Joan started to cross the bridge into the town, she was stopped by the town captain, who was in the process of selling it to the Burgundians. Joan and her army stayed in a field with no provisions. From there, they traveled to Château-Thierry, where they stayed until August 1. While there, Joan asked the king to exempt the villages of Domrémy-la-Pucelle and Greux from taxation, and he agreed.

The arrival of the Duke of Lorraine gave Joan a great boost, and the army continued to the northern end of Paris, where they set up camp. On August 15, the Duke of Bedford rode out and proposed battle. Joan was ready to fight but was also wary of a trap. The 8,000 to 9,000 English soldiers and 6,000 to 8,000 Burgundian soldiers were hidden behind ditches and wagons. Approximately 7,000 French soldiers watched Joan try to entice the English out into the open, but they could not be lured. At daybreak the following day, the English left for Paris.

King Charles went to his comfortable residence in Compiègne, a few miles northeast of Paris. Joan pleaded with him to take Paris, but La Tremoille had become insistent that Charles listen to him. Charles still remembered the awful massacre of 5,000 people in Paris when the Burgundians took over the city and was likely unwilling to see such a repeat.

Joan was given permission to travel south to Paris with La Hire and the dukes of Alencon and Bourbon. Little did she know that Charles, in his negotiations with Philip the Good, had agreed to vacate the towns she had just captured in exchange for a four-month truce. Philip, in the meantime, was negotiating with the English for titles to Brie and Champagne in exchange for more of his soldiers.

On September 8, the king finally allowed Joan to attack Paris. It was Joan's most unsuccessful day in battle. During the long wait, her troops had lost some of their enthusiasm, and she could not seem to rally them. Then, when she was hit in the leg by an arrow, the king ordered her to withdraw. Mary Gordon wrote, "Because [Charles] had no real personal loyalty to her, because he was interested only in what she could represent, when her representations failed to be of use to him, she ceased to exist as important, or perhaps, even real."[2]

When Joan's army was forced to disband on September 21, instead of going home to Domrémy-la-Pucelle she stayed with the court. The waiting was awful. In late November, Charles told her she could try to take the town of La Charité-sur-Loire, but first she had to conquer the small village of Saint-Pierre-Le-Moûtier. She had few men with her. Although they eventually took Saint-Pierre-Le-Moûtier, the siege at La Charité was long and unsuccessful. She did, however, have some good news at this time: Her family had been ennobled. While she had never pursued such honors, and had in fact refused ennoblement for herself, she accepted it for her brothers. The king's act, however, worried her. Was he trying to rid himself of her by paying her off? She returned to court feeling like a failure. Her power was on the wane. The soldiers were unpaid or underpaid and did not have enough provisions. Many had deserted.

The voices of St. Catherine and St. Margaret had told her that she would be captured before midsummer. Joan must have been distressed, but she carried on and went to Lagny. A miracle occurred at Lagny that would be passed down through the ages and led to her eventual canonization: Joan brought a baby back to life long enough for it to be baptized and buried in consecrated ground.

Also in Lagny, she captured a man named Franquet d'Arras, who was a known Burgundy sympathizer. Joan decided to exchange him for another man and offered him up for ransom. When she learned that the other man had died, she changed her mind and took d'Arras to trial. After confessing to his crimes, he was decapitated. Joan had broken a promise, which in the unwritten laws of chivalry, was a terrible wrong. To many she had acted out of character, and it became a mark against her.

CAPTURE AT COMPIÈGNE

By March 1430, King Charles was beginning to understand that the Duke of Burgundy was not acting in good faith, but the king still did not change his tactics. Charles had promised his cousin the Duke of Burgundy to give up Compiègne, which had a good vantage point for attacking Paris. The duke, in exchange, was supposed to vacate Paris, which he had not done. Charles was being duped, of course, which he later admitted in a letter dated May 6, 1430.

Rumor spread that the townspeople of Compiègne were going to fight the English rather than face being turned over to them. They were under siege and desperate. Joan, moved that they were willing to risk their lives in order to remain French, rushed to their aid, reaching the town on May 15. After eight days, the standoff with the Burgundians was proving to be too much. They had thousands of soldiers to Joan's hundreds. She planned a surprise attack when they were resting, which gave her a slight advantage for a short time.

The Burgundian captain, Jean de Luxembourg, sent his troops to meet the maid. Despite having only a handful of men, Joan kept making assaults against the town. In the meantime, Burgundy's men joined de Luxembourg, as did a large number of fresh English troops. Joan's men begged her to retreat, but it only made her angry. Because she could not rally them the way she had months before, they fled to the safety of the town. Once they were within the gates, the governor, in a panic, raised the drawbridge. Joan was left outside the gate with only a few of her men. She and her horse became mired in a muddy field, and an archer grabbed the flaps of her "beautiful gold and scarlet surcoat"[3] and yanked her from her horse. Joan had worried about treason, and many wondered if someone had turned against her. The truth would never be known.

Joan was captured by the Bastard of Wandomme and taken to Margny, along with her brother Pierre, Jean d'Aulon, and a few others. The Duke of Burgundy went to see her and put her in the care of Jean de Luxembourg. From there she was taken to a prison at Beaulieu.

Shown above, *The Peasant Maid of Orleans in the Hands of the English*, by Ronald Wheelwright. Captured by the Burgundians and sold to the English, Joan would find herself not being ransomed as a prisoner of war (as was then the custom), but put on trial as a heretic.

For a year—from late April 1429 until the end of May 1430—Joan of Arc's remarkable success on the field of battle had given hope to the French and struck fear in her enemies. Now, her capture was proof to her enemies that she was not invincible. De Luxembourg was willing to have her ransomed if she would agree to stop fighting the Burgundians. One witness said that she refused. The English wanted her badly. The vicar general of the Inquisition, a high-ranking official in the Catholic Church who favored the English, asked that she be sent to Paris for trial on grounds of heresy—a religious crime in which the accused is believed to hold beliefs that defy the teachings of the church. The day after her capture, faculty members of the University of Paris wrote to the Duke of Burgundy to ask that she be handed over for trial as a heretic. Though the word *sorceress*, or *witch*, was not used in their request, it was implied.

"It was among the richest, the most learned, the most privileged, the highest of England and of France that the terror of heresy and the practice of witchcraft took its firmest hold,"[4] according to biographer Marina Warner. Joan's victories, the rumors of her voices and her prophecies, and the great influence she had over Charles and the French frightened them. In their minds, the devil was at work in the form of Joan the Maid.

RANSOMED

Jean de Luxembourg decided to ransom Joan, though he took his time. Pierre Cauchon, the bishop of Beauvais, saw an opportunity to retaliate against the maid who had inspired thousands. He offered various sums of money, and de Luxembourg eventually settled on £10,000. While the negotiating continued, Joan was allowed to have her steward Jean d'Aulon with her, but after she attempted to escape by lifting up the floorboards in her room, she was put in a dark cell alone. There, she again acted against the code of chivalry by attempting escape. It was understood that if one gave one's word (in this case not to escape), it must be honored. She defended herself by saying that she had not given her word that she would not attempt escape. The truth was that she would rather have died than become a prisoner of the English.

Jean de Luxembourg then moved Joan to his château at Beaurevoir, where she met his wife, Aunt Jeanne, and possibly his stepdaughter, all of whom became her supporters. She tried to escape again by leaping out of a tower window and fell 60 to 70 feet (18 to 21 m). She did not break any bones, but she was badly bruised. Mary Gordon wrote, "This is another proof of Joan's incredible health, strength, and powers of recuperation. It could also be another instance of her youthful belief that she could take great risks and not be hurt by them."[5] She was also full of remorse for her action, for her voices had told her not to attempt it.

Was Jean de Luxembourg hoping that King Charles would bid against the English and save the maid? If so, it was not to be. Charles, true to his character, did not act. No counteroffer was made. Joan was sent to the Duke of Luxembourg's city home at Arras, and handed over to the English in November 1430. On November 21, the rectors of the University of Paris wrote to King Henry VI to say that she was in their power. Cauchon arranged to have her tried as though she were in his territory in Beauvais, which was against the laws that were in place, but no one heeded them.

On January 3, 1431, Joan was officially taken by the English. Her trial, however, was to be not a military trial but an ecclesiastical, or religious, one, and Pierre Cauchon was to conduct the interrogation and the hearing. This was bad news indeed. The future did not bode well for Joan the Maid.

Sentenced
to Death

The trial was held in Rouen, an English-controlled city in Normandy. It took eight months for the preliminary trial to begin in the chapel of Rouen Castle. Before the trial, Joan had to undergo another virginity test, with the Duchess of Bedford, Anne of Burgundy, in charge. It is likely that she forbade the guards from raping Joan. Cauchon sent scouts to Joan's hometown to find anything the judges could use against her, but they returned with glowing reports of the girl, which he made sure were not put in the records.

When the trial finally began in February 1431, the interrogation segment did not get off to a good start; in fact, parts of it were embarrassing for Pierre Cauchon. The inquisitor, Jean Graverent, was not present; the information that was going to be used against Joan came from anonymous sources, which meant it could have been made up; and Joan had not yet been formally charged with anything. It was up to the judges to decide what charges to bring against her.

POLITICS AND RELIGION

It was obvious that Cauchon wanted to rid himself of the girl who had caused so many problems for him and for his allies in the church, but there was more involved than his own personal agenda. Although the Great Western Schism had ended in 1415 and Pope Martin V in Rome was now the only pope, it did not keep the University of Paris from trying to win back the power they had with the pope in Avignon. In fact, the University of Paris faculty wanted their General Council to rule the entire Catholic Church alongside the papacy and wanted the French national assembly to become as powerful as the British Parliament. But their plans were ruined because Joan's victories not only gave power to Charles but also weakened the council's already waning influence on the papacy.

THE JUDGES' INVESTIGATION BEGINS

In 1184, the Catholic Church began using trials known as Inquisitions to investigate and punish heresy. Later, as these investigations grew, the use of torture was employed to force suspected heretics to confess their crimes or to convert nonbelievers. Like other Inquisitions, the purpose of Joan's trial was to determine if she had broken church laws. Mary Gordon wrote, "By the time he was ready to begin, Cauchon had assembled one cardinal, six bishops, thirty-two doctors of theology, sixteen bachelors of theology, seven doctors of medicine, and one hundred other clerical associates."[1] All were sympathetic to the Anglo-Burgundian cause, not to the papacy in Rome. Joan viewed the men

In this 1824 painting by Paul Delaroche, Joan of Arc is interrogated in her cell by the cardinal of Winchester, who sought to brand her as a fraud for political reasons.

before her as Burgundians and English, not as the authority of the church. They were, in fact, her enemies. In her mind, the pope in Rome was the sole authority.

Joan was the only female present. She started by stating her name, that she was born in Domrémy, that her father was Jacques d'Arc and her mother Isabelle, and that she was about 19 years old. It was obvious from the beginning that she was not afraid. She refused to swear on the Holy Gospels that she would be truthful in her answers. When ordered to say the *Pater Noster* (the Our Father, a basic Christian prayer), she cleverly answered the bishop that if he would hear her in confession she would oblige. At one point she said she would tell the pope everything, but they said he was too far away. They also recognized that the pope would likely not hear her for fear that he would anger the English.

Told by the judges to swear on the Holy Gospels that she would tell the truth, she replied, "I do not know on what you may wish to question me. Perhaps you may ask such things as I will not answer."[2] She was proving to be a challenge for the judges with her stubbornness, her quick answers, and her lack of self-pity. Cauchon worried that she would gain sympathy.

HER VOICES

It was during this phase of the trial that Joan named St. Catherine and St. Margaret as the voices that had directed her. St. Catherine of Alexandria, Egypt, was a Christian maiden who was beheaded by Emperor Maximinus for converting the Romans to Christianity and for refusing his hand in marriage. Joan grew up hearing about her, as she was the patron saint of young girls and also the patron of Maxey-sur-Meuse, a parish near her hometown. St. Margaret of Antioch was a maiden who also tried to convert the Romans to Christianity and was beheaded for her work. Joan had no doubt seen her statue in Domrémy-la-Pucelle many times. Later, Joan added St. Michael the archangel. She said, "It was St. Michael whom I saw before my eyes, and he was not alone but was well accompanied by angels of heaven . . . I saw them with the eyes of my body as well as I see you; and when they left me I wept and wished that they would have taken me with them."[3]

Did Joan not know that she was putting herself in danger when she spoke of communicating with the world beyond? She was clear in her testimony that God was speaking directly to her. What she did not understand was that the church had

WITCHES AND HERETICS

As much as they might have liked, the judges at Joan of Arc's trial could not declare her a witch or sorceress because they did not have enough evidence. They were terrified of sorcery or witchcraft: "The Catholic Church had established in the early 1300s that they should try those who were practitioners of ritual magic, as well as heretics."* Two women were burned at the stake in Paris in 1390–1391 for having dealings with the devil, which they only confessed to after being tortured. In the next century, witch trails became common across Europe.

"Witches were believed to gather together and conjure supernatural phenomena in a group . . . female sorcery was considered to be a communal activity."** During her trial, the judges made note of the fact that Joan believed in sharing her visions. Necromancy (speaking with the dead), sorcery, alchemy, and even astrology were all considered crimes punishable by the Catholic Church.

Joan's judges started out trying to prove that she had practiced magic by asking her questions based on information their scouts had collected. They wanted to know about the children's ritual of very specific teachings about angels and demons. Angels did not have substance, and if they could be touched and smelled, they belonged to the lower realm of demons. Further, the church had specific teachings about hearing voices. Because Joan had never confessed to a priest or higher authorities about her voices, she was listening to them without church permission. The judges remained fixated on sorcery and witchcraft. The trial was turning into a witch hunt.

dancing around the fairy tree in her village. Fairies, always considered female, could tell a person's fate. The judges claimed that it was a sin that she had reportedly brought a baby back to life. They were even suspicious of the butterflies that were said to have flown around her banner during a battle. "Butterflies, like toads and lizards, symbolized dead souls."*** Because Joan's battle wounds never slowed her down, this too made the judges suspicious. The word got back to them that she had predicted that she would be wounded, which added to their belief that she was a sorcerer. They accused her of carrying lucky charms and amulets, which she denied.

From the moment it was decided to try Joan as a heretic, she stood little chance of saving her life. They were terrified of her power, and that fear made them despise her. After Joan's death, many other women would be burned at the stake for the same reason.

---

*Marina Warner, *The Trial of Joan of Arc*, p. 18.
**Ibid., p. 17.
***Ibid., p. 22.

CROSS-DRESSING

The next line of questioning concerned Joan's masculine attire. There was a clause in church laws that allowed women to dress in men's clothes in order to protect themselves, but the judges viewed Joan's outfit that resembled that of a knight as offensive. Her hair was cut short, and she wore a man's jacket, long laced leggings, a short mantel that went to her knees, a cap, and thick boots. Because of this, she was accused of making an idol of herself.

Joan had been wearing men's clothing since she stayed in Vaucouleurs. No one at the time had objected to her clothes or that she called herself Joan the Maid—not even the king. The most obvious reason for wearing men's clothing was to protect herself, both when she formed her army and now in prison. She was terrified of being sexually assaulted while incarcerated. She even gave up what was most precious to her—attending Mass and receiving Communion—in order to avoid the possibility of being violated. She was barely successful, as attempts were made. She also never was allowed a minute alone. Finally, she agreed to wear women's clothes if allowed to go to Mass, but would not do so when in her cell. Later she said that she would "not for anything take the oath that she will not take up arms or wear male dress to do our Lord's will."[4] She began to contradict herself, saying at one point that her voices had commanded her to wear male dress and later that the issue was unimportant.

Aware that her interrogators were her enemy, Joan knew she had to concentrate deeply on their questions, as her responses might save her life. It was hard to prepare, however, for there were many trick questions. For example, when they asked her who the true pope was, she replied, the pope who was in Rome. It was an honest answer, but one that may have been a mark against her, as the English judges had always been on the side of the Avignon pope.

The tower in Rouen, constructed in 1205 by King Philip II of France, was where Joan of Arc was imprisoned and tortured during her trial. It has since become known as the Joan of Arc tower. During one of her escape attempts, she leaped from a similar tower.

Joan slept and ate little, as circumstances at the prison were horrible. She should have been put in the archbishop's prison, where she would have been guarded by women and given better treatment. Cauchon got around that rule by having three court members, all clerics, hold the three keys needed to unlock her cell door. Contrary to the standards set for a church trial, Joan was treated as a prisoner of war, forced to wear leg irons and guarded by five men, three of whom stayed inside her cell and two outside the door. She had to remain focused during hours and days of intense questioning, in spite of her time spent in a dark cell, placed in irons, and in danger of being raped. She was completely alone, with no one to defend her.

Under these extraordinary circumstances, she never veered from her one absolute truth: God was her supreme authority. Her judges, however, believed they were the intermediaries of God and that she did not have the right to go directly to God. As evidence of their authority, they pointed to a new hierarchy of the church that had been created by the University of Paris. The rules stated that "the Church Militant was the Catholic Church on earth; the Church Triumphant was the church in heaven; the Church Suffering was those of its members in purgatory."[5] The men before her were the Church Militant. They could not make an error or a false judgment. In essence, she must put them first. If she refused, she could be accused of not submitting to the church. Joan maintained that she was in the hands of God: "It is my sense that it is all one, God's and the church's, and that there should be no difficulty about it. Why do you make difficulties about its being one and the same thing?"[6]

When asked if she thought she was in a state of grace, which meant that God had forgiven her sins, she answered, "If I am not, may God put me there. And if I am, may God keep me there, for I would be the most sorrowful woman in the world if I knew that I was not in the grace of God."[7] Gordon wrote, "It is remarkable that she kept her composure, her good humor, her health, and her freshness of thought and diction."[8]

After three weeks, little progress had been made. Cauchon grew impatient. Anyone sitting in the courtroom must have been impressed with Joan's performance, which further infuriated Cauchon. On March 10, he decided to make the trial private and moved the questioning to her cell. This was an effective move, because Joan began to lose focus. On March 17, Joan was asked if God hated the English. She replied, "Of the love or hate which God has for the English and of what He does to their souls, I know nothing; but well I know that they will be driven out of France, excepting those who will die there, and that God will send victory to the French over the English."[9]

The judges became more accusatory than questioning. They asked about her going to battle on the Feast of the Ascension; they brought up the fact that she had put a man to death after promising him life. Her attempted suicide came up. The constant questioning soon wore Joan down.

On March 13, when an interrogator named Jean de La Fontaine asked, "Why you, rather than another?" Joan replied, "It pleased God to do so through a simple maiden, to humble the king's enemies."[10]

Throughout the judges' investigation, clerics recorded statements made in French and translated them into Latin. The judges intervened even here, changing the clerics' logs as they saw fit. Some of the clerks left out Joan's answers as they recorded the trial. Still, many remarked on Joan's extraordinary clarity and memory throughout her ordeal.

NEW ACCUSATIONS

The second phase of the inquiry, the ordinary trial, started on March 26. Seventy articles of accusation were brought up, but they were reduced to 12 key crimes. Some of them were:

> [H]er visions of the saints and their speaking to her in French and promising to lead her to paradise; the sign the crown prince had received when she spoke with him in private; her predictions of future events; her insistence on wearing male attire; her leap from the tower; and her statement that she had done everything in God's name.[11]

Still, the court members were not unanimous in what the charge should be. Some thought that wearing men's clothes was a "thin basis for condemnation,"[12] as was lack of submission to the Church Militant, which was a new law, and one they suspected Joan did not fully understand.

IN HER OWN WORDS

A prayer Joan uttered during her trial is an example of the way she communicated with God:

> Very sweet God, in honor of Your Holy Passion, I beg You, if You love me, that You reveal to me how I should answer these men of the church. I know well, regarding my clothes, the command that I received, but I do not know anything about the manner in which I should drop it. On that, may it please You to instruct me.*

* Régine Pernoud and Marie-Véronique Clin, *Joan of Arc: Her Story*, p. 121.

At the same time, frustration mounted over Joan's insistence that she obeyed only God. On May 9, the authorities took her to the tower of the castle and threatened to torture her. She flatly told them that under no circumstances would she tell them anything else, but if she did, she would say it had been forced out of her. This caused confusion as some of the men did not want to go through with it, but then their confusion fueled their anger. Around this time, Cauchon received word from his superiors that the trial was taking too long. On May 19, Cauchon told Joan that the masters of the University of Paris had rendered their verdict. After a 14-month trial, she was found guilty for wearing masculine dress and for heresy because she claimed she answered to God and not to the Catholic Church. In her defense, she said, "As for my words and deeds, which I declared in the trial, I refer to them and will maintain them."[13] She added that if "she saw the fire and the faggots lit and the executioner ready to kindle the fire, and she herself were in it, she would say nothing else and would maintain till death what she said in the trial."[14]

JOAN RELENTS

On May 24, the verdict was publicly announced. Joan was led outside for the first time in months, where she was to be excommunicated, but first she had to listen to a sermon. She had asked that her report be sent to Rome, but that request was denied. Dressed in women's clothes, she stood on a high scaffold as her head was shaved. She was asked if she would repent, give up men's clothes, and stop fighting. Additionally, she would have to submit to the Catholic Church. This repentance was called an abjuration, a document she would have to sign. Joan laughed—whether because she was nervous or defiant will never be known. In the past, when her signature was needed, she had been known to draw a cross—a symbol that the document should be considered null and void. This time she drew a circle, but someone took her hand and made her draw a cross, though she knew how to write her name. Joan thought her repentance would set her free. Instead, Cauchon sentenced her to life in the same prison where she had spent the last five months, which was a living nightmare. She was a young woman, a woman of God, doomed to a living hell.

Once a prisoner had signed an abjuration, if she committed the same error again, she could be condemned to death. Cauchon knew that the chances of Joan remaining in women's clothing were slender, for to do so would invite sexual assaults. A few days later, Joan was seen in men's clothing. A commonly held belief is that someone stole her dress and she had no choice but to don the male clothing that had been left for her.

RELAPSE TRIAL AND DEATH

After hearing of Joan's supposed defiance, Cauchon and the vice inquisitor went to the prison. Cauchon demanded to know if she had heard her voices. Joan admitted that she had. He wanted to know what they said. She replied, "God has expressed through St. Catherine and St. Margaret His great sorrow at the strong treason to which I consented in abjuring and making a revocation to save my life, and said that I was damning myself to save my life."[15]

The assessors were called together on May 29 to determine Joan's fate for being insubordinate to the Church Militant. Of the 42 men gathered, 39 of them thought the *cedula*, a document explaining the definitions of the Church Militant, should be read to her again. Only three voted to turn her over to a secular court. Because Cauchon considered the three mere consultants, he refused to go to a secular court and delivered Joan to be burned at the stake.

When Friar Martin Ladvenu announced her fate, Joan "began to cry out sorrowfully and pitiably to tear and pull her hair."[16] Surprisingly the bishop of Beauvais allowed her to take Communion. According to Gordon, "If she was excommunicated [from the church], she would have been denied the sacraments . . . proof that Cauchon knew he was acting in bad faith."[17] Dressed in a long black shift, she walked in chains to the marketplace in Rouen on May 30. On her head was a hat with words that read, "heretic, relapsed apostate, idolator." The crowd, which included 700 to 800 soldiers, jeered. She cried when she saw the high mound of sticks. The guards led her up a flight of stairs, where she was tied to the stake. She requested that a crucifix be held before her eyes, and "an English soldier tied together two sticks for her, which she kissed, and put in her garment."[18]

Friar Ladvenu ran up with a golden crucifix he had found in a nearby church and held it in front of her. As the flames crept up around her she cried out "Jesus!" six times. The excited mob, after hearing her cries, grew sober. The executioners, who sometimes stabbed prisoners to death rather than have them endure the pain of burning, had been instructed to keep her as far from the flames as they could to make her death more painful. She suffered horribly.

After she was declared dead, her charred body was displayed before those who wanted to see for themselves if she was indeed a female. Once they were satisfied, the executioners started a big fire around her body, and her remains were burned to ashes. Brother Ysambard de la Pierre, a Dominican friar, reported what he saw years later at her rehabilitation trial:

And the executioner said and affirmed that, in spite of the oil, the sulphur, and the charcoal which he had applied to the entrails and heart of the said Joan, in no way could he burn them up, nor reduce them to ashes either the entrails or the heart, which he found amazing, like an obvious miracle.[19]

Rehabilitation
Trial

When her many supporters learned that Joan had been burned at the stake, they were deeply grieved. But little was known about exactly what had occurred during her trial at Rouen, as the city was under English rule. As far as her French supporters knew, the church had conducted the trial in a traditional way. The English, naturally, were relieved to have it all over and done.

In December 1431, the Duke of Bedford organized a coronation for Henry VI at Notre-Dame Cathedral in Paris. The Duke of Burgundy refused to attend the coronation, a sure indication that if he had not already shifted his loyalty to the French he was considering it. In fact, he had signed a six-year truce with King Charles's ambassadors. To the Duke of Bedford's surprise, Henry's uncle, Cardinal Beaufort, who had anointed him, demanded that Bedford resign as regent of England and France. The inner structure of the English political system was undergoing change, but no one was quite sure if it meant a reversal of fortune for the French.

The city where Joan had died, Rouen, continued to be held by the English, until an uprising occurred on February 3, 1432. Led by a man called Ricarville, 104 men, believing they would receive support from French reinforcements who never arrived, sought to kick the English out of the city. They were all later beheaded. On the French end of things, Georges de La Tremoille, whose advice kept the king in a state of apathy and indifference, was stabbed in the stomach by a distant relative of the king who thought his assassination would have positive results for Charles. The overweight La Tremoille survived because his size prevented the sword from hitting an organ. He then fled the court in 1433.

After peace was announced between France and Burgundy on September 20, 1435, the French sought to rid their nation of the English.

In 1436, an armed revolt against the English government occurred in Paris. Arthur de Richemont and Joan's old friend Dunois placed the city under siege; eventually supporters inside the city let down ladders to allow them in. They entered Paris on April 13, 1436, as Joan's prosecutor, Pierre Cauchon, fled. Joan's prophecy that the English would lose everything in France within a seven-year period was unfolding.

Life improved for France, in fits and starts. King Charles arrived in Paris a year later, on November 12, 1437, accompanied by his son, the dauphin Louis. The conquest of Paris, however, did not mark the end of the fighting between the two nations. Then, between 1438 and 1439, a plague broke out in Paris, killing 50,000 citizens. The Duke of Orleans's ransom was paid, at last, in 1440, as another of

Joan's goals had come to pass. Although King Charles's soldiers captured some small cities in 1441, Charles, discouraged, began to focus on a new mistress and a life of pleasure. In 1444, Henry VI married Margaret of Anjou, the daughter of the Duke of Anjou, and a truce was signed with England, which would turn out to be temporary. Joan's old companions, La Hire and Dunois of Orleans, began a successful campaign in Normandy in 1444. In 1449, Charles, newly inspired, started a siege in Louviers, an important town. Then an insurrection against the English in Rouen that same year overthrew them after 30 years of occupation. Charles entered the capital of Normandy on October 29, 18 years after Joan was burned at the stake.

In the meantime, Henry VI was trying to raise the funds—even going so far as to pledge the crown jewels—to raise another army to enter France. But Arthur de Richemont's army was ready when the English army entered Cherbourge in 1450. On April 15 of that year, the English

IN HER OWN WORDS

Before her death, Joan of Arc prophesized the end of the English conquest of France:

> And before seven years are done the English will have left behind a greater stake than they did before Orleans; they shall lose everything in France. And the English will have a greater loss than they ever had in France. And that will be through a great victory which God will send the French.*

*Joan of Arc Quotes/Joan of Arc Resource. http://www.joan-of-arc-resource-com/quotes.html.

were defeated, and northern France finally belonged to King Charles. When Bordeaux fell to French forces in 1451, the nation was entirely free of the English.

TENSION BETWEEN SECULAR AND SPIRITUAL GROUPS

Popular sentiment around Joan grew as time passed. People spoke of her heart that could not be burned to ashes and of a dove that was seen flying over her as she died. Joan, more than anyone before her, had made the people feel patriotic toward France. Then, Pope Nicholas V sent a lawyer to King Charles in August 1451, suggesting a rehabilitation trial for Joan.

The king asked a man named Guillaume Bouille to investigate. In 1452, he reported, "What a disgrace for the royal throne it would be if in the future our adversaries could repeat that the king of France had kept a heretical woman in his army!"[1] Like many other medieval monarchs, King Charles sought to diminish the power of the church in his kingdom and to strengthen his own power and that of his loyal nobles. Despite this, Charles opened an inquiry into Joan's death, but it was short-lived. The church could not admit that killing Joan had been a mistake, even if it had been done for obvious political reasons. The church was considered the highest authority, and could, theoretically, also decide if Charles was a legitimate king. But there was another problem. Because Joan had been tried for heresy, the clerics who judged her found themselves in a peculiar situation, for if they admitted they had been wrong, it would force them to acknowledge their unfairness and prejudice. Pope Nicholas V realized that he and the king needed each other. They decided to give amnesty to all who testified, which meant they would not be held accountable for their actions during Joan's earlier trial.

THE LONG NULLIFICATION TRIAL

Most of the original judges who had condemned Joan were dead, including Pierre Cauchon and Joan's prosecutor, who had drowned in a sewer. In April 1452, 21 people testified on Joan's behalf. The initial inquiry demonstrated that the degree of prejudice displayed during her original trial was so great that it was suggested that that trial could be voided. It had been "a political trial in which, by convicting Joan of heresy, the English had successfully sought to destroy the woman in whom they saw, not without reason, the instrument of Charles VII's victories and coronation."[2] The pope, however, was not happy with the outcome and asked the French inquisitor, Jean Brehal, to reopen the trial instead. Brehal came up with the idea to appeal to Joan's mother and her two sons, making it a private trial. This trial was to be as weighted in Joan's favor as her own trial had been weighted against her.

An inquest, however, was delayed another three years, during which time Pope Nicholas died. He was replaced by Pope Calixtus III, who, in 1455, agreed to the petition of the d'Arc family. The goal again was to annul Joan's previous sentence.

The case was opened on November 7, 1455. Joan's mother, Isabelle Romee, was brought from Orleans, where she and her sons were living under the protection of the king. Isabelle was asked to introduce the case in the Cathedral of Notre-Dame in Paris. She wanted her family's name to be cleared, and King Charles cleverly used her request to reopen the case. By using Joan's family to make the case a private one, if the outcome was positive, both Joan's honor and the king's would be restored.

Joan's mother's opening speech was full of emotion—so much so that after she finished speaking, she fainted. She said, in part:

By my legal marriage, I brought into the world a daughter, whom I duly caused to receive the honour of the sacraments of baptism and confirmation, whom I brought up in the fear of God, respectful and faithful . . . Then, although she had not thought, or plotted or done anything not according to the faith . . . envious persons wishing her evil . . . embroiled her in an ecclesiastical trial . . . wickedly condemning her at the last and burning her.[3]

It was December 12 before the trial started. After five days, the actual minutes of the 1431 trial were produced. The archbishops of Paris and Reims, along with the inquisitor, agreed to be judges. Months passed as 101 articles to be discussed were written up and submitted, and then boiled down to 27. They called over 100 witnesses, all of whom gave favorable accounts of Joan.

What was at issue at Joan's previous trial, along with the heretical act of wearing men's clothes, was "her willingness to trust her voices rather than what her judges told her she should believe."[4] If those voices were viewed by the judges as opposed to Catholic doctrine, then those questions should have been addressed to the pope, which did not happen in Joan's case. In the 24 years since Joan's death, a change in church doctrine stated that "a devout Catholic has a duty to obey the Holy Spirit,"[5] especially when that person's life was judged to be holy.

The case brought by Isabelle Romee and Joan's brothers, Pierre and Jean d'Arc, was pronounced in the name of the Holy Trinity on July 7, 1456. The accusations against Joan were deemed false. The archbishop of Reims, various bishops, and the Dominican priest, Jean Brehal, one of two inquisitors in France, recommended that the case against Joan of Arc be annulled. A general procession

Tried for heresy and sorcery, Joan of Arc was burned at the stake in the marketplace of Rouen on May 30, 1431. In this illustration, she holds a makeshift cross of two sticks tied together while a priest holds a crucifix.

followed, and the decision posted in two squares in Rouen, including Vieux-Marche, where Joan had been burned at the stake.

The decision meant that Charles VII had been right to believe in Joan. Following the verdict, the king granted a coat of arms to her brothers. It was "an enduring mark of his esteem, which sealed his approval and created a faction deeply interested in rescuing her name."[6] Two years after the trial, Joan's mother died on November 28, 1458, knowing her daughter's name had been cleared.

JOAN'S FRIENDS AND FOES AFTER HER DEATH

King Charles, though considered by many to be a traitor to Joan of Arc and an ineffective king, did mature somewhat after Joan died. In 1435, he signed the Treaty of Arras, which helped to reconcile the Burgundians and the Armagnacs. He also consented to the nullification trial of 1450 to 1456, which cleared Joan's name—and his. He then created an army that would become the gendarmes of France and reduced the political influence of the Catholic Church in his nation. His son, Louis XI, would rule France from 1461 to 1483 and would grow into a more effective leader than his father had been.

In 1458, John, the Duke of Alencon, was found guilty of treason to the king and was locked away. When Charles VII died in 1461, John was freed by the king's son, Louis XI. Louis, however, wanted the control of the duke's children, to marry them off as he saw fit, and he wanted three of the duke's fortresses. After the duke refused, he was kept in prison, where he died on July 18, 1474. Joan's old comrade, John, the Count of Dunois, Bastard of Orleans, went on to win many battles in the name of the king, but he quarreled with Louis XI and was dismissed from court. He died on November 23, 1468.

Joan's brother, Pierre, was taken prisoner before Joan was and had to sell his wife's inheritance to pay his ransom. He followed a woman named Madame des Armoises, who claimed to be the reincarnation of Joan of Arc, during part

EAN · CONTE · DE · DVNOIS
AS TARD · D'ORLEANS · MORT · LAN · 14

In this miniature portrait from circa 1630, John, the Count of Dunois, is shown. The French patriot and martyr was a loyal companion of Joan of Arc.

of 1436, probably hoping to receive some money from the king, but she confessed to being an imposter, and that ended it. Pierre then moved to Orleans, where the duke gave him a home to make up for his years in captivity and offered him financial help. Joan's other brother, Jean, went back to Domrémy-la-Pucelle and married his niece. He held important posts in various towns and lived a relatively long life.

After his downfall in 1433, Georges de La Tremoille was banished from court in 1453 and died in 1466. John, the Duke of Bedford and former regent of England, died in Rouen in 1435. Though he was known to be merciful to prisoners, he did nothing to help Joan, and in fact supported everything Pierre Cauchon did. Up until the very end, he had the power to save her life, but he chose not to.

King Henry VI of England married Margaret of Anjou in 1445, and they had one son, Edward, who was killed in battle. Henry tried to hold on to the dual monarchy of France and England but failed. In 1453, his inherited mental illness made him unable to lead. In 1460, Richard, the Duke of York, captured the king and forced the king to acknowledge him as the rightful heir to the English crown. Richard's son, Edward IV, eventually became king after defeating Henry's army in 1461, and Henry and his wife were exiled to Scotland but were later captured and locked in the Tower of London until 1470. He managed to rule again for a very short period, but after Edward died, he was sent back to the Tower of London, where he was murdered on May 21, 1471.

Cauchon went to Rouen, where, because the clergy did not like him, he was given a much lesser role as bishop of Lisieux in 1432. He went on to a moderately successful career and remained loyal to the English. He died while being shaved at his home on December 18, 1442. After his death, he was rejected by all the descendants he left behind, who publicly declared their innocence in regard to Cauchon's part in Joan of Arc's trial.

Saint Joan

Joan's reputation rode the political and religious tides in France for decades. The power of the Catholic Church continued to wane in France as the country's political system went from monarchy to republic. The French Revolution, which started on July 14, 1789, culminated in the first French republic in 1792. Joan's star faded during this era. Timothy Wilson-Smith wrote, "The French Revolution swept away its royal family in the year that it swept away the cult of Joan."[1] She was perceived as Catholic and royalist, and not at all in step with the new secular and democratic republic. It was during this time that a bronze statue of her in Orleans was melted down to build a cannon.

Another outcome of the French Revolution was that priests who remained loyal to papal authority were persecuted.

Pope Pius VI was forcibly brought to France from Rome in 1798, when the French Republican army occupied that city. Then in 1799, Napoleon Bonaparte became first consul of France after staging a coup d'etat (overthrow of government). He reinstated Roman Catholicism as the state religion. Napoleon assured Catholics that they could practice their faith, but he made sure in an 1803 agreement with the pope that his own power remained strong. Soon known as Napoleon I, he became the self-proclaimed emperor of France in 1804, even taking the crown from Pope Pius VII and placing it on his own head. By 1809, Napoleon tried to bring the church completely under his control, but Pope Pius, who remained in exile in France until 1814, refused to cooperate.

AN APPEAL FOR SAINTHOOD

In 1803, the bishop of Orleans requested of Napoleon that the festival of Joan of Arc be revived. Napoleon wrote that

> there is no miracle that French genius cannot achieve when national independence is threatened . . . the French nation has never been vanquished, but our neighbors . . . constantly sowed in us the dissension from which came the calamities of the period in which the French heroine lived.[2]

Napoleon's answer was a resounding yes. With the revival of the festival of Joan of Arc, a new interest in medieval history took hold.

In 1815, after Napoleon was defeated at the Battle of Waterloo, the French monarchy was reestablished. Various Bourbon kings—Louis XVIII, Charles X, and Louis-Philippe, the Duke of Orleans—ruled for a short time. The July Monarchy, which lasted from 1830 to 1848 under Louis Philippe, arose after Charles X gave up his power in 1820.

The French emperor, Napoleon Bonaparte, is shown in this 1812 painting by Robert Lefèvre. During his reign, Napoleon revived the Joan of Arc festival, after the radical government during the French Revolution had banned it.

Under the constitutional monarchy that Louis-Philippe established, politics became more liberal as he tried to dissolve some of the power of the aristocracy in order to give more to the growing bourgeoisie, or middle class.

In 1849, Felix Dupanloup was named bishop of Orleans, a position he held for 29 years. He took charge of the Joan of Arc festival. He preached in 1869:

> In her I find everything that moves me, including the name of Orleans, that has become mine since God called me to be the bishop of your souls; I like the peasant simplicity in her origins, the chastity in her heart, her courage in battle, her love for the land of France, but above all the holiness in her life and death.[3]

He had even heard an English Protestant call Joan a saint. Dupanloup sent a petition to Rome, requesting sainthood for Joan. Timothy Wilson-Smith wrote, "Joan stood for a stable national destiny . . . Joan symbolized the nation at its best."[4]

Ironically, as the power of the Catholic Church was weakening, Joan of Arc provided a much-needed lift for it. Since about 1859, the power of the Catholic Church had been challenged by "modernism, a habit of mind that was secular, rationalist, and anti-hierarchical."[5] The church thought Joan could bring back many who had gone astray. She was a great example of all a true Christian could be.

FRANCO-PRUSSIAN WAR

Before Dupanloup's request could be granted, Napoleon III and the French army entered into a war with Prussia and the German states on July 15, 1870. They were defeated by Otto von Bismarck, who had cleverly united the Germans in their hatred of France. The Germans had suffered defeat during the Napoleonic Wars, and they wanted revenge. Though it was a short war (July 15, 1870, to February 1, 1871), it changed European history, creating a strong and united German Empire. It also marked the end of France's Second Empire. To the horror of the French, Alsace-Lorraine, land of Joan of Arc, now belonged to the Prussians. The French vowed to get it back, no matter how long it took. The Third Republic of France, based at Versailles, with Napoleon III in power, lasted 70 years. The constitutional laws of the new republic were established in February 1875.

SACRÉ-COEUR

In 1873, after its defeat to the Prussians, the conservative French government decided to build a church dedicated to the Sacred Heart of Jesus, which would be called the Basilique du Sacré-Coeur. They wanted to honor their pledge to build a church if Paris was not damaged by the Prussians. With a striking Roman-Byzantine design, it was also a guilt offering, as their belief was that France's defeat by the Prussians was due to the sins of the people. The French had a much stronger national identity as a result of their humiliating defeat, and who better to represent them than Joan of Arc?

The church is situated majestically at Montmartre, the highest point in Paris. A mosaic called *Christ in Majesty*, which includes Joan of Arc and the Virgin Mary, is one of the largest in the world. Two large bronze equestrian statues dominate the church entrance—Joan of Arc strides one horse, and King Louis IX, who was born in 1215 and became a saint, the other.

As early as the 1870s, people had begun to make pilgrimages to Joan's home in Domrémy-la-Pucelle. The number of printed works about her had increased dramatically, and more people were reading her inspiring and tragic story. Even French soldiers were taught the story of Joan of Arc. In 1874, Dupanloup again started to make inquiries about making Joan a saint of the Catholic Church.

The same year, a sculptor named Emmanuel Frémiet designed and erected a statue of Joan of Arc in Paris at Place des Pyramides, which represented Joan's new place in the consciousness of the French people. The main home of France's rulers, Tuileries Palace, had been burned down during the Prussian invasion, and the statue of Joan on a horse holding high her banner had a huge impact: "Glistening in the sun, it would inspire the nation to recapture Lorraine, and, if Joan could not yet be called a saint, she was the heroine who would ride out to inspire the soldiers of France,"[6] wrote Timothy Wilson-Smith. Joan of Arc became an obsession of the French people.

SAINT JOAN

The man who succeeded Dupanloup, Bishop Couillie, picked up where Dupanloup had left off. All through the 1880s, he sent inquiries to Rome about making Joan a saint. The cardinals in Rome passed them on to Pope Leo XIII. On January 27, 1894, he signed the so-called introduction of her cause for beatification.

Couillie was replaced by Bishop Touchet, who went to Rome in 1896, and a year later was asked to begin a study of Joan's sanctity, or virtues. There were problems. In recommending someone for sainthood, Mary Gordon wrote, "emphasis is placed upon the three theological and four moral virtues: it is assumed that the candidate would have kept the Ten Commandments of Moses and the six commandments of the church—the latter having to do with questions of fidelity to worship."[7] She continues, "The three virtues are faith, hope, and charity; the four morals are prudence, justice, fortitude, and temperance."[8]

The devil's advocates, whose job was to argue against the canonization, were torn. (*Devil's advocate* is a term used to refer to someone who offers an opposing view from the one being spoken or written.) Some argued that Joan was admired for political rather than religious virtues, which

SAINTHOOD

Beatification is a term used by the Catholic Church to refer to the church's recognition of someone who lived a holy life. It is usually the first step toward becoming a saint. Canonization is the process by which someone is found to be a saint. Pope John XV developed the official canonization process in the tenth century. It was revised most recently by Pope John Paul II in 1983. He took out the "devil's advocate" part of the process. It can take centuries to become a saint, which was the case with Joan of Arc. Until Mother Teresa, whose canonization process began two years after her death in 1997, the minimum amount of time in which sainthood could be bestowed was five years.

Other steps include the following: A local bishop looks for heroic virtue in the candidate's life and writings, and that information is sent to the Vatican. Theologians and cardinals evaluate the life of the candidate. The pope declares that the candidate is a role model of Catholic virtues. In order to be a candidate for beatification, the honored person must be responsible for a posthumous miracle. (Those who died for a religious cause, or martyrs, do not have to bestow a miracle.) To become a saint, there must be proof of a second posthumous miracle. Joan was responsible for a miracle that happened on August 22, 1909, in Lourdes, France, during the Blessed Sacrament. A woman named Therese Belin lay unconscious, desperately ill with a form of tuberculosis. Monsignor Leon Cristiani, who wanted to see Joan canonized, obtained permission from the bishop of Orleans to bring forth Joan of was a legitimate concern. She was accused of being disobedient to her parents for not telling them about her voices, the advocates were concerned that various men had seen

Arc during the blessing of the sick. "At the first invocation to Blessed Joan of Arc, Therese opened her eyes, at the second she sat up on her stretcher and at the third she felt she had been cured."* Another woman was healed of "perforating plantar affliction,"** a condition that had caused a hole to form in the sole of her foot.

Mary Gordon wrote in an article titled "Desperately Seeking Joan" that "'saint' connects immediately to 'goodness.'"*** People go to saints because they feel a special connection with them, or because they feel like someone is cheering them on. Saints offer inspiration. Approximately 3,000 people have been canonized by the Catholic Church. "It's not the pope who makes a person a saint," Gordon wrote. "He recognizes what God has already done."**** She summed up Joan of Arc's saintliness: "Joan of Arc was a virgin and she died for what she believed, but she does not fit the type of the virgin martyr. Ardent, impatient, boastful, resistant, implacable, she is like all great saints, a personality of genius."*****

---

*"What Were the Miracles That the Vatican Accepted to Raise Joan of Arc to the Official Rank of Canonized Saint?" St. Joan Center. http://www.stjoan-center.com/FAQ/question7.html.
**Ibid.
***Mary Gordon. "Desperately Seeking Joan—Woman Behind the Hype—Joan of Arc." Commonweal, March 10, 2000.
****Ibid.
*****Ibid.

In this oil-on-canvas portrait from 1865 by Sir John Everett Millais, the spiritual side of Joan of Arc is highlighted. Calls for Joan's canonization grew steadily during the nineteenth century.

her breasts, and they were uncomfortable with her boasts about her chastity. They even brought up her refusal to answer questions the judges had asked at her trial and wondered whether her jump off a seven-story tower had been an act of suicide. Could her voices have been the "result of a hysterical delusion?"[9] Again, in order for Joan to achieve beatification, she had to be a model for the faithful.

The devil's advocates questioned whether or not she had saintly fortitude. She had attempted to escape from prison, complained when given her sentence, and cried when she was brought to the stake. She was definitely not a martyr in their eyes, because she did not want to die, especially when she abjured, or repented.

ROME DECIDES

Bishop Touchet took the results of his research back to Rome, where the conclusion reached by the bishops of Orleans was studied. The Roman bishops then dismissed negative evidence. They saw a virtuous young woman "who would bring the wandering sheep back into the fold . . . they forgot their devotion to obedience and conformity and created a saint who is full of contradictions and imperfections that make, if not a saint, then a great and lovable human being."[10] On January 6, 1904, Pope Pius X proclaimed that Joan of Arc was beatified. The formal ceremony took place on April 18, 1909, at St. Peter's Basilica in Rome. Joan had passed the first step in her journey to sainthood.

Touchet wanted her to be canonized, and he spent all of his time and energy to make it happen. Touchet presented his findings on April 17, 1914. Pope Pius X died shortly afterward. On September 3, 1914, Pope Benedict XV agreed to a canonization trial. He approved the results on July 6, 1919, and the ceremony took place on May 16, 1920.

Joan and the Arts

Over centuries, Joan of Arc has been exhaustively depicted in the arts. By 1894, more than 400 plays and musical works had been created. Much of what was written in the century after Joan's death was biased, depending on the author's point of view. For example, Joan is featured in William Shakespeare's *Henry VI, Part I*, written between 1592 and 1594, as a holy woman who turns into a witch. Biographer Mary Gordon wrote, "Her sorcery is the only possible explanation for British defeat at the hands of the militarily inferior and generally spineless French."[1] At the end of the play, she tries to save her skin by claiming to be pregnant.[2]

In France, however, Christine de Pizan wrote "Song in Honor of Joan of Arc" when Joan was still alive, and the *Story of the Siege of Orleans* was dramatized in Orleans four years after her death. At the end of the fifteenth century, Augustinian friar Philip of Bergamo wrote of Joan's many wonderful qualities. One engraver even made a small woodcut portrait of Joan as a Greek maiden. Because Homer and Virgil and Ovid were widely read by the educated during the medieval era, the women depicted in these stories, such as the goddess Diana in Virgil's *Aeneid*, helped to make Joan "the most modern and the most famous of European heroines,"[3] according to historian Marina Warner. She added, "Feminism was more alive then than it would be for 300 years."[4]

"The representation of Joan's image in painting, sculpture, literature, music and popular culture from the Age of Enlightenment to the Second Republic will be shown to offer a brilliant, if perhaps at times distorted, mirror of the forces in French society that called forth her memory according to their bidding,"[5] wrote Nora Heimann, author of *Joan of Arc in French Art and Culture (1700–1855): From Satire to Sanctity*.

By the eighteenth century, Joan was the object of political satire. It was the era of the Enlightenment, a movement in Western Europe that stressed reason and science in philosophy. French philosopher Voltaire wrote a mocking poem called *The Maid of Orleans*, which outraged many, but was widely read. Of Voltaire's poem, reviewers Alia Nour-Elsayed and Petra ten-Doesschate Chu of Seton Hall University wrote:

> Joan is an illegitimate stable girl who is protected by a saint and his winged companion against many suitors and sexual assailants, including members of the church and both British and French royalty. It was his way of criticizing the French monarchy and

the Catholic Church and the emphasis they placed on virginity as a virtue.[6]

By the time the Bourbon monarchy was reestablished in 1815, Joan had been transformed from the classical woman warrior into "the embodiment of heroic and pious suffering" in literature and sermons and paintings and had a "high symbolic value for the restored monarchy and the Catholic Church."[7] From 1830 to 1848, artists became obsessed with the image of Joan of Arc. King Louis-Philippe decided to make the grand palace of Versailles a museum, and one of the paintings selected was *The Consecration of Charles VII at Reims, 17 July, 1429* by Auguste Vinchon. Joan of Arc stands in the center of the painting. The king's daughter, Marie d'Orleans, had also created several sculptures of Joan. Then in the 1840s, French scholars began the first honest analysis of Joan of Arc. Soon after, French historian Jules Michelet began writing an accomplished biography of Joan. Through his work, Joan was again perceived as a French heroine.

In America, Mark Twain wrote a fictional memoir that was published in 1896 titled *Personal Collections of Joan of Arc* by *The Sieur Louis de Conte (Her Page and Secretary)*, which he considered his favorite work. While it never had the success of his other books, it helped introduce Joan of Arc to American audiences.

THEATER

Between 1800 and 1870, 34 plays based on Joan of Arc's life were written. Johann Christoph Friedrich von Schiller's work *The Virgin of Orleans* was first performed in 1801 in Leipzig, Germany, and influenced many writers over the next century. He made Joan into a romantic heroine. In von Schiller's story, an enchanted helmet prevents Joan from falling in love, but she falls for an English soldier anyway. Once captured by the English, she casts off her chains, rushes back into battle, and is fatally wounded. Needless to say, playwrights of the day ignored historical facts when creating their heroines. In 1896, Charles Peguy—a resident of Orleans who had turned away from the Catholic Church and had heard the stories of Joan all his life—completed the first part of a three-part play about her, which was not successful. Peguy returned to the church in 1909 and revised the play.

Seventeen plays were written about Joan in 1909, the year she was beatified. Twenty-nine plays were written about her between the two world wars. Irish playwright George Bernard Shaw wrote *Saint Joan*, which was performed in New York in 1923. Shaw presented an entirely different Joan, one who was young, sure of herself, and filled with high spirits. In the play, Joan struggles against church and state, a theme that related to Shaw's own life in Ireland.

In 1930, German expressionist author Bertolt Brecht wrote the Marxist-themed drama *Saint Joan of the Stockyards*. Although based on Joan's life, the play was set in working-class Chicago. In 1953, Jean Anouilh wrote *The Lark*, about the French collaboration with the Germans during World War II. Music in the film was composed by Arthur Honegger. In other lesser-known works, Joan has been portrayed as an alien sexual being and has been the subject of a fantasy novel, action/adventure novels, psychological novels, a one-woman lesbian play, and a science-fiction novel.

PAINTINGS AND SCULPTURE

We are reminded by biographer Mary Gordon that "artists' choices are based on what suits their gifts and their convictions about what is important in the world."[8] In an essay, Mark Twain wrote:

> How strange it is!—that almost invariably the artist remembers only one detail—one minor and

meaningless detail of the personality of Joan of Arc: to wit, that she was a peasant girl—and forgets all the rest; and so he paints her as a strapping middle-aged fishwoman, with costume to match, and in her face the spirituality of a ham . . . The artist should paint her spirit—then he could not fail to paint her body aright. She would rise before us, then, a vision to win us, not repel: a lithe young slender figure, instinct with "the unbought grace of youth," dear and bonny and lovable, the face beautiful, and trans-figured with the light of that lustrous intellect and the fires of that unquenchable spirit.[9]

A large number of portraits of Joan exist, many of which use the same themes in depicting the French heroine. Most center around one of three images: "the visionary, the war-rior, or the martyr."[10] The first likeness of Joan was a small pen sketch drawn by Clement de Fauquembergue in 1429. He was the Burgundian notary of the Parliament of Paris, and obviously hostile toward the maid, whom he had never seen in person. He created a sexy Joan, wearing a low-cut, tight-fitted dress, with her hair falling loosely down her back. She held a sword and a standard. Nora Heimann pointed out that "for a woman to wear her hair loose indi-cated an immodest woman. Prostitutes were portrayed with unbound and uncovered hair. It could also mean an unmar-ried status."[11] The image served as a standard, however, all through the Middle Ages and the Renaissance.

Peter Paul Rubens painted *Joan of Arc at Prayer* in 1620 with flowing red hair down to her waist. He could be excused for his mistake, for the public did not have access to her records until the 1840s, when it was learned that Joan wore her hair cropped above her ears. Jean-Auguste-Dominique Ingres, however, knew Joan wore her hair short like a boy's when he painted the coronation of Charles VII in 1854, yet he put her in a skirt and gave her long hair, making her more goddess than soldier. Called *Joan of Arc at the Coronation of Charles VII at Reims,* Joan stands at the composition's "still centre, her soft flesh set against the hard, gleaming armour, her lustrous eyes cast up to heaven, standing with one hand on the altar, the other holding her standard."[12] Another famous painter, John Everett Millais, painted her in prayer in 1865. All the artists seemed resistant to a Joan of Arc with cropped hair wearing men's clothes. Joan of Arc museums can be found in Vaucouleurs and in Chinon, which was the king's residence while he waited to be crowned king.

Seventeen sculptures of Joan stand in places such as the Jardin du Luxembourg; Place des Pyramides; Place St. Augustin in Paris and Reims, France; Fairmount Park in Philadelphia; Riverside Park in New York City; French Market and St. Louis Cathedral in New Orleans; in Portland, Oregon; Montreal, Canada; and the Smithsonian American Art Museum. The first monument to her was erected on the bridge in Orleans in 1502. Public sculptures of her were common between 1870 and 1940, the most famous being Emmanuel Frémiet's equestrian statue at the Place des Pyramides. As with portraits, after Joan was canonized in 1920, thousands of statues of her appeared all over France.

DID YOU KNOW?

The Bible discusses women's hair in the First Letter of Paul to the Corinthians, 11:3–15. St. Paul stated that "Christian women wear their hair long and veiled as a sign of their obedience, modesty, and submission to man."

MUSIC

Joan was also a natural subject for opera, where characters are larger than life. In 1803, Jacques Offenbach wrote an opera about her; then in 1845, Giuseppe Verdi wrote perhaps the most famous of the operas using Joan as the subject, *Giovanna d'Arco*. Charles Gounod wrote the opera *Jeanne d'Arc* in 1873 and Pyotr Ilyich Tchaikovsky dedicated *La Pucelle d'Orleans* to Joan in 1879. In 1945, Paul Claudel wrote the text and composer Arthur Honegger composed the music for an oratorio titled "Joan at the Stake," which has been performed all over the world.

FILM

Directors started making films about Joan of Arc in 1898. Cecil B. DeMille made *Joan the Woman* in 1917, and another film, starring the English actress Sybil Thorndike and based on the play by George Bernard Shaw, was made in 1927. But it was the silent film *La Passion de Jeanne d'Arc*, made in 1928 by Danish director Carl Dreyer, that is, according to one critic, "the greatest film about suffering ever made."[13] The camera shifted to show in stark reality the evil faces of Joan's prosecutors as they wore her down. The beautiful, tormented face of the Italian actress playing Joan, Maria Falconetti, in a series of close-ups, is unforgettable. According to Mary Gordon, the actress was "nearly psychologically destroyed"[14] by the filming of it, and in fact never made another film. *La Passion de Jeanne d'Arc* did not meet with critical success, but in 1995 "it was named by the papal paper *Osservatore Romano* one of the greatest religious films of all time."[15]

In 1948, Ingrid Bergman played Joan in Victor Fleming's *Joan of Arc*. Another film, *Saint Joan*, based on the George Bernard Shaw play, was made in the United States in 1957. Directed by Otto Preminger and with Jean Seberg in the lead role, Joan is depicted as courageous and faithful, but

The actress Renee Maria Falconetti is shown in a scene from *La Passion de Jeanne d'Arc*, a 1928 French film directed by Carl Dreyer. The film is considered one of the great adaptations of Joan's life.

for many, the acting was not up to par. Between 1989 and 2005, nine feature films or television movies were made featuring Joan of Arc. As recently as 1999, Leelee Sobieski, Peter O'Toole, and Olympia Dukakis were in Christian Duguay's *Joan of Arc*. Perhaps the most dramatic is *The Messenger*, directed by Frenchman Luc Besson, which did not win favorable reviews. Joan is represented as "a rebellious, sacrilegious, deluded, short-tempered and argumentative teenager."[16] Mary Gordon quoted the film's star Mila Jovovich, who played Joan: "Joan was really a mover and a shaker. She was a real Tasmanian devil."[17]

FESTIVAL OF ORLEANS, FRANCE

Perhaps the greatest tribute to Joan of Arc is the commemoration of her at Orleans. From the time she saved Orleans from the British, who departed on May 8, 1429, she has been celebrated and honored, except for one brief lapse of 18 years. Once Joan's trial was officially nullified, the cardinal of the city was enthusiastic about the celebration that traditionally took place on May 8. In fact, Orleans provided for Joan's mother, Isabelle, until her death in 1458.

The mystery play *The Siege of Orleans*, thought to be written by Jacques Millet, was first performed in Orleans in 1435. It boasts 146 speaking parts and takes at least two days to perform. It is a pageant beyond comparison. As previously mentioned, between the French Revolution and 1803, the festival was not held. When Napolean allowed it to be held again, the mayor requested that a new monument be built in Joan's honor. Traditionally, the part of Joan had been played by a boy, *le puceau*, or boy virgin; it was 1912 before a young woman was given the privilege of playing Joan of Arc.

POLITICAL SYMBOL

America was an ally to France during World War I, which started in 1914, and during that time U.S. soldiers became fascinated by the woman warrior. It was not long before she became an icon for American war purposes. In a print ad that was popular at the time, a shapely woman wearing a helmet and holding up a sword encourages "women of America" to buy savings stamps to support the war effort. At the top of the ad the words "Joan of Arc Saved France" are printed. Joan's image was also used to "attack the Germans for bombarding Reims and damaging the cathedral where Charles was crowned king."[18] By the end of World War I in

Shown here, people in medieval costumes march in an annual procession celebrating the feast of Joan of Arc in Orleans, France.

1918, the German republic had to return lands, including Alsace-Lorraine, to France. Joan again became a symbol of national unity.

During World War II, Joan of Arc became a figurehead for both sides within France—the Free French and the puppet Vichy French government living under German rule. One poster that was pro-German showed the city of Rouen burning under attack from Allied bombs, with Joan

REPLICA OF JOAN OF ARC STATUE IN NEW ORLEANS

An exact replica of the Joan of Arc statue at Place des Pyramides in Paris was sent to New Orleans in 1958 as a gift from the people of France. It was put in storage because New Orleans could not come up with the $35,000 needed to erect it. When French president Charles de Gaulle visited New Orleans in 1960, he personally got involved and had four French cities and the people of New Orleans raise the money together. By 1972, a 17-foot (5-m) base pedestal had been built in the Place de France, and the statue of Saint Joan was put on top of it. In 1999, the statue was moved to the French Market, or Vieux Carré, on the corner of Saint Philip and Decatur streets. Three flags—American, French, and the state flag of Louisiana—fly behind it.

In October 1998, a playwright and event planner named Amy Kirk came up with the idea of having a procession to honor the unofficial patron saint of New Orleans, Joan of Arc. It was to take place on Twelfth Night, or January 6, Joan of Arc's birthday, and the start of New Orleans's Carnival season. Kirk explained that Joan of Arc represents "defiance, courage, virtue . . . and, especially since Hurricane Katrina, she represents strength and tenacity. It's a perfect time for a warrior saint to come lead our city."*

The first procession in Joan's honor was held on January 6, 2009. The Joan of Arc Project was founded to great fanfare on May 8, 2009, commemorating Joan lifting the siege of Orleans, France. It is a secular organization that presents an annual parade, celebrates French holidays, keeps an active Joan of Arc book club going, and inspires the public to visit the statue.

Since Hurricane Katrina devastated New Orleans in 2005, photographer John Michael Craven has called the New Orleans statue of Saint Joan of Arc "Beacon of Hope."

---

*Molly Reid. "A New Parade Honoring Joan of Arc Joins the Phunny Phorty Phellows to Kick Off Carnival," Nola.com. http://blog.nola.com/mollyreid/2008/12/a_new_parade_honoring_joan_of.html.

of Arc burning at the stake. The French Resistance (an underground operation fighting the Germans) had as its symbol Joan of Arc holding the cross of Lorraine. Charles de Gaulle, who would become president of France after the war ended, carried the cross of Lorraine with him.

Legacy

Timothy Wilson-Smith summed up the paradoxes in Joan of Arc's life. He said:

> A girl condemned in 1431 by a French court was rehabilitated by the nullification of that verdict in 1452–56, and then, after a much longer process, in 1920 canonized as a saint of the Catholic Church. . . . This belatedly canonized saint was also declared by the Church to be the patroness of France and given a public holiday by the secular French State, while at the same time she was greatly admired in the English-speaking world, where in her lifetime she would have found her most determined enemies.[1]

Though Joan's feats were superhuman, she was completely human. Like any teen today, she had a streak of stubbornness, and at times was impatient and impulsive. She was also kind and compassionate, radiating a quality of grace that had even the toughest knights dropping everything to follow her. Perhaps it was they—especially Jean d'Alencon and La Hire—who knew her better than anyone. They slept near her at night when on the battlefields, and they watched her incredible bravery as she went forward to meet the enemy. Her faith and her courage when she was held captive helped her through a trial that had doomed her before it started.

HER VOICES

Perhaps the most extraordinary thing about Joan of Arc is her obedience to her voices. It is also the part of her that is most often analyzed: Was she insane? Was she deluded? Was she schizophrenic? Francoise Meltzer, professor and chair of comparative literature with an appointment in the Divinity School at the University of Chicago, said, "It [the 1400s] was a time when there was no division between the body and the mind, when martyrs like Joan had a conviction which they enacted through their bodies as if they were vessels for their beliefs."[2]

Joan heard her voices and acted. In *Joan of Arc: From Heretic to Saint*, Donald Spoto wrote:

Many people, even those sympathetic to Francis [St. Francis of Assisi] and Joan, maintain that in a new age informed by depth psychology, such things as stated simply do not happen. The lives of Francis of Assisi, and Joan of Arc—indeed, the lives of Isaiah, Jesus of Nazareth, Buddha, and Muhammad—make little sense without reference to the world of the spirit, with reference to the living God, who may disclose Himself as He wishes, to whom He wishes, under what circumstances He wishes. All were addressed by what might be called the world beyond—by a presence that could not be ignored. . . . The ordinary limitations of language, which describe common experiences, have to be broken; there is, after all, no direct equivalent for an inner experience of such overwhelming power— invariably so overwhelming, in fact, that it alters one perception of life and its purpose. Such was the experience of Joan of Arc.[3]

FREEDOM

The strong faith of the people in the countryside of France in the 1400s made miracles quite acceptable. Children were imbued with religious faith. Joan, like the other children, was trained in the teachings of the church when she was a child and heard many stories from the Bible and other sources that spoke of miracles.

To Joan, freedom of the individual was important. The ability for an individual to choose right from wrong is a basic part of Christianity. One aspect of her that infuriated the men chosen to judge her was her insistence that she was free to communicate directly with God, which they believed she was not allowed to do. Freedom was a strong theme in Joan's life, involving both personal and social liberty. According to Jane Marie Pinzino in "The Condemnation and Rehabilitation Trials of Joan of Arc," it is freedom in three senses: "the political freedom of a people, the spiritual freedom of the individual, and the perfect freedom of God."[4] When she was at Poitiers, she wanted to liberate the French people; at her own trial, "her own spiritual liberty was at stake."[5] At the rehabilitation trial, "belief in the freedom of God to save his people was foundational. Moreover,

A sculpture in Domrémy-la-Pucelle, Lorraine, France, depicting Joan of Arc. The Roman Catholic Church recognized the French national heroine as a saint in 1920.

the heart of the matter was faith in God's freedom to choose a simple young woman, instill in her a passion for human freedom and grant her the power to make it real."[6]

Joan is no longer "in the forefront of French minds,"[7] according to Wilson-Smith. He added, "In 1948 11 per cent of those asked put her [Joan] in a list of famous French men and women; in 1980 that figure was 2 per cent, in 1989 zero per cent of the French people in general, however, take Joan for granted, and the young scarcely know her."[8] She is thought to be better known in the United States than in Europe. Perhaps university and college curriculums across the United States that include women's studies have something to do with it. Wilson-Smith wrote, "She is now a figure of universal significance as a feminist model, if not a model feminist."[9] Young women are aware, even today, that the qualities of self-confidence and independent judgment in women can cause suspicion, and sometimes punishment.

Françoise Meltzer said Joan of Arc "blurred the boundaries between masculine and feminine, between obedience and incredible courage, and we live in a time when we are very interested in that."[10] She added that she believes the answer to Joan's continuing popularity "lies in the uncertainty of the times in which we live."[11] Jeremy du Quesnay Adams wrote in his preface to the book *Joan of Arc: Her Story*, "One need not be a French nationalist, or a Christian, or a feminist to find Joan of Arc fascinating and her treatment by the several male establishments of her time an outrage."[12]

DID YOU KNOW?

The television series *Joan of Arcadia*, which ran from 2003 to 2005, was about a teenage girl's conversations with God. The teen, played by Amber Tamblyn, finds herself wondering if she is sane as she tries to follow God's directives while trying to live a normal American teenage life. The writer and creator of the show, Barbara Hall, was obsessed with Joan of Arc as a child growing up in Virginia. Brought up a Methodist, both she and her sister eventually converted to Catholicism as adults.

Rose Pacatte. "Joan of Arcadia: An Interview with Its Catholic Producer." American Catholic. http://www.americancatholic.org/Messenger/Mar2005/Feature1.asp.

Régine Pernoud, who has written several books on Joan of Arc, wrote in *Joan of Arc: By Herself and Her Witnesses*: "It remains true that, for us, Joan is above all the saint of reconciliation—the one whom, whatever our personal convictions, we admire and love because, over-riding all partisan points of view, each one of us can find in himself a reason to love her."[13]

CHRONOLOGY

1412 or 1413	Joan of Arc born in Domrémy-la-Pucelle, France, on or about January 6.
1424	First heard voices at age of 12.
1428	Joan goes to Vaucouleurs, meets Robert de Baudricourt; attack on Joan's village; Joan accused of breaking a vow of marriage.
1429	Second meeting with de Baudricourt on February 12; departs for Chinon to meet dauphin Charles on February 22; arrives in Chinon and meets Charles in early March; Joan enters Orleans on April 29; English raise the siege and depart Orleans on May 8; Joan on Loire campaign on way to Reims on June 8; Battle of Patay on June 18; Joan convinces Charles to be crowned in Reims on June 25; Charles VII's coronation on July 17; attack on Paris on September 8; Joan told to abandon attack on September 9; army breaks up on September 21.
1430	Capture of Joan at Compiègne on May 23; from May to November, Joan held prisoner in various castles; Burgundians turn Joan over to English for ransom in November; arrives as prisoner in Rouen, an English stronghold, in late December.
1431	Joan appears for the first time in court on February 21; explanation of charges on May 23; abjuration, or repentance, on May 24; wears men's clothes and relapse trial opens on May 27; Joan burned at stake on May 30.

1449   Charles VII decides to ask for new trial for Joan.

1453   The Hundred Years' War ends.

1455   Pope Calixtus III authorizes new trial.

1456   Former trial nullified. The Catholic Church overturns Joan's conviction and declares her to be a martyr.

1909   Joan of Arc officially beatified by Pope Pius X.

1920   Joan recognized as a saint by Pope Benedict XV on May 16.

NOTES

CHAPTER 1

1. Mary Gordon, *Joan of Arc*. New York: The Penguin Group, 2000, p. 64.
2. Régine Pernoud and Marie-Véronique Clin, *Joan of Arc: Her Story*. New York: St. Martin's Press, 1998, p. 44.
3. Marina Warner, *Joan of Arc: The Image of Female Heroism*. New York: Alfred A. Knopf, 1981, p. 71.
4. Mary Gordon, *Joan of Arc*, p. 35.
5. Warner, *Joan of Arc: The Image of Female Heroism*, p. 62.
6. Ibid., p. 70.
7. Régine Pernoud and Marie-Véronique Clin, *Joan of Arc: Her Story*, p. 64.

CHAPTER 2

1. Marina Warner, *Joan of Arc: The Image of Female Heroism*, p. 35.
2. Mary Gordon, *Joan of Arc*, p. 11.
3. Régine Pernoud and Marie-Véronique Clin, *Joan of Arc: Her Story*, p. 162.
4. Marina Warner, *Joan of Arc: The Image of Female Heroism*, p. 25.
5. Mary Gordon, *Joan of Arc*, p. 15.
6. Marina Warner, *Joan of Arc: The Image of Female Heroism*, p. 119.
7. Ibid.
8. Ibid., p. 122.
9. Ibid., p. 26.

CHAPTER 3

1. Régine Pernoud, *Joan of Arc: By Herself and Her Witnesses*. Lanham, MD: Scarborough House, 1982, p. 35.

2. Mary Gordon, *Joan of Arc*, p. 37.
3. Marina Warner, *Joan of Arc: The Image of Female Heroism*, p. 23.
4. Mary Gordon, *Joan of Arc*, p. 39.
5. Timothy Wilson-Smith, *Joan of Arc: Maid, Myth and History*. London: The History Press, 2008.
6. Allen Williamson, "Biography of Joan of Arc." http://www.joan-of-arc.org/joanofarc_biography. html.
7. Mary Gordon, *Joan of Arc*, p. 35.
8. Ibid., p. 40.
9. Ibid., p. 43.
10. Ibid.
11. Timothy Wilson-Smith, *Joan of Arc: Maid, Myth and History*, p. 31.
12. Ibid.
13. Régine Pernoud, *Joan of Arc: By Herself and Her Witnesses*, p. 58.
14. Ibid.
15. Régine Pernoud and Marie-Véronique Clin, *Joan of Arc: Her Story*, p. 31.
16. Ibid., p. 225.

CHAPTER 4

1. Régine Pernoud and Marie-Véronique Clin, *Joan of Arc: Her Story*, p. 220.
2. Ibid., p. 13.
3. Ibid., p. 14.
4. Marina Warner, *Joan of Arc: The Image of Female Heroism*, pp. 160–161.
5. Timothy Wilson-Smith, *Joan of Arc: Maid, Myth and History*, p. 35.
6. Régine Pernoud and Marie-Véronique Clin, *Joan of Arc: Her Story*, p. 41.

7. Ibid.
8. Ibid., p. 49.
9. Ibid., p. 55.
10. Ibid., p. 172.
11. Ibid.
12. Ibid.
13. Ibid., p. 59.
14. Ibid., pp. 67–68.

CHAPTER 5

1. Mary Gordon, *Joan of Arc*, p. 69.
2. Ibid., p. 70.
3. Ibid., p. 79.
4. Marina Warner, *Joan of Arc: The Image of Female Heroism*, p. 97.
5. Mary Gordon, *Joan of Arc*, p. 100.

CHAPTER 6

1. Mary Gordon, *Joan of Arc*, p. 105.
2. Ibid., p. 107.
3. Régine Pernoud and Marie-Véronique Clin, *Joan of Arc: Her Story*, p. 113.
4. Mary Gordon, *Joan of Arc*, p. 116.
5. Régine Pernoud and Marie-Véronique Clin, *Joan of Arc: Her Story*, p. 122.
6. Ibid.
7. Ibid., p. 112.
8. Mary Gordon, *Joan of Arc*, p. 120.
9. Régine Pernoud, *Joan of Arc: By Herself and Her Witnesses*, p. 174.
10. Régine Pernoud and Marie-Véronique Clin, *Joan of Arc: Her Story*, p. 118.
11. Timothy Wilson-Smith, *Joan of Arc: Maid, Myth and History*, p. 74.

12. Ibid., p. 126.
13. Régine Pernoud and Marie-Véronique Clin, *Joan of Arc: Her Story*, p. 129.
14. Ibid., p. 133.
15. Ibid.
16. Ibid.
17. Mary Gordon, *Joan of Arc*, p. 128.
18. Ibid., p. 129.
19. Timothy Wilson-Smith, *Joan of Arc: Maid, Myth and History*, p. 127.

CHAPTER 7

1. Marina Warner, *Joan of Arc: The Image of Female Heroism*, p. 188.
2. Régine Pernoud, *Joan of Arc: By Herself and Her Witnesses*, p. 259.
3. Mary Gordon, *Joan of Arc*, p. 133.
4. Timothy Wilson-Smith, *Joan of Arc: Maid, Myth and History*, p. 86.
5. Ibid.
6. Régine Pernoud and Marie-Véronique Clin, *Joan of Arc: Her Story*, p. 176.

CHAPTER 8

1. Timothy Wilson-Smith, *Joan of Arc: Maid, Myth and History*, p. 172.
2. Ibid., p. 176.
3. Ibid., p. 183.
4. Ibid., p. 180.
5. Mary Gordon, "Desperately Seeking Joan: Woman Behind the Hype, Joan of Arc." *Commonweal*, March 10, 2000.
6. Timothy Wilson-Smith, *Joan of Arc: Maid, Myth and History*, p. 187.

7. Mary Gordon, "Desperately Seeking Joan."
8. Ibid.
9. Ibid.
10. Ibid.

CHAPTER 9

1. Mary Gordon, *Joan of Arc*, p. 161.
2. Timothy Wilson-Smith, *Joan of Arc: Maid, Myth and History*, p. 162.
3. Marina Warner, *Joan of Arc: The Image of Female Heroism*, p. 202.
4. Ibid., p. 219.
5. Nora M. Heimann, *Joan of Arc in French Art and Culture (1700–1855): From Satire to Sanctity.* Surrey, UK: Ashgate Publishers, 2005, p. 12.
6. Alia Nour-Elsayed and Petra ten-Doesschate Chu, "H-France Review: Joan of Arc in French Culture (1700–1855): From Satire to Sanctity." http://www. h-france.net/vol6reviews/nourelsayedandchu.html.
7. Ibid.
8. Mary Gordon, *Joan of Arc*, p. 149.
9. Mark Twain, *Joan of Arc*. San Francisco: Ignatius Press, 1896, appendix, p. 452.
10. Régine Pernoud and Marie-Véronique Clin, *Joan of Arc: Her Story*, p. 242.
11. Nora M. Heimann, *Joan of Arc in French Art and Culture (1700–1855): From Satire to Sanctity*, p. 12.
12. Timothy Wilson-Smith, *Joan of Arc: Maid, Myth and History*, p. 181.
13. Mary Gordon, p. 149.
14. Mary Gordon, p. 150.
15. "Saint Joan of Arc." http://csis.pace.edu/grendel/ WS5/JoanofArc/essayonjoan.html.
16. Ibid.

17. Mary Gordon, *Joan of Arc*, p. 165.
18. Timothy Wilson-Smith, *Joan of Arc: Maid, Myth and History*, p. 207.

CHAPTER 10

1. Timothy Wilson-Smith, *Joan of Arc: Maid, Myth and History*, p. 48.
2. Françoise Meltzer, "Joan of Arc Fever." http://magazine.uchicago.edu/0012/research/invest-joan.html.
3. Donald Spoto, *Joan of Arc: From Heretic to Saint*. San Francisco: HarperCollins, 2007, pp. 24–25.
4. Jane Maria Pinzino, "The Condemnation and Rehabilitation Trials of Joan of Arc," International Joan of Arc Society. http://smu.edu/ijas/pinzino.html.
5. Ibid.
6. Ibid.
7. Timothy Wilson-Smith, *Joan of Arc: Maid, Myth and History*, p. 216.
8. Ibid., p. 221.
9. Ibid.
10. Françoise Meltzer, "Joan of Arc Fever."
11. Ibid.
12. Régine Pernoud and Marie-Véronique Clin, *Joan of Arc: Her Story*, p. xv.
13. Régine Pernoud, *Joan of Arc: By Herself and Her Witnesses*, p. 277.

BIBLIOGRAPHY

Gordon, Mary. *Joan of Arc*. New York: The Penguin Group, 2000.

Heimann, Nora M. *Joan of Arc in French Art and Culture (1700–1855): From Satire to Sanctity*. Surrey, UK: Ashgate Publishers, 2005.

Pernoud, Régine. *Joan of Arc: By Herself and Her Witnesses*. Lanham, MD: Scarborough House, 1982.

Pernoud, Régine, and Marie-Véronique Clin. *Joan of Arc: Her Story*. New York: St. Martin's Press, 1998.

Spoto, Donald. *Joan of Arc: From Heretic to Saint*. San Francisco: HarperCollins, 2007.

Twain, Mark. *Joan of Arc*. San Francisco: Ignatius Press, 1896.

Warner, Marina. *Joan of Arc: The Image of Female Heroism*. New York: Alfred A. Knopf, 1981.

———. "Introduction." In *The Trial of Joan of Arc*. Evesham, UK: Arthur James, 1996.

Wilson-Smith, Timothy. *Joan of Arc: Maid, Myth and History*. Gloucestershire, UK: The History Press, 2006.

WEB SITES

"Joan of Art Quotes." Joan of Arc Resource. Available online at http://www.joan-of-arc-resource.com/quotes.html.

Lanhers, Yvonne, and Malcolm G.A. Vale. "Joan of Arc, Saint." History.com. Available online at http://www.history.com/topics/saint-joan-of-arc.

Pinzino, Jane Marie. "The Condemnation and Rehabilitation Trials of Joan of Arc." International Joan of Arc Society. Available online at http://smu.edu/ijas/pinzino.html.

Reid, Molly. "A New Parade Honoring Joan of Arc Joins the Phunny Phorty Phellows to Kick Off Carnival." NOLA.com. December 30, 2008. Available online at http://blog.nola.com/mollyreid/2008/12/a_new_parade_honoring_joan_of.html.

"Sacré-Coeur Basilica, Paris," Sacred Destinations, August 23, 2009. Available online at http://www.sacred-destinations.com/france/paris-sacre-coeur.

S.A.S. "Joan of Arc Fever." University of Chicago Magazine. December 2000. Available online at http://magazine.uchicago.edu/0012/research/invest-joan.html.

Williamson, Allen. "Biography of Joan of Arc (Jehanne Darc)." Joan of Arc.org. Available online at http://www.joan-of-arc.org/joanofarc_biography.html.

———. "St. Joan's Notable Quotations: French to English Translations of the Famous Sayings of Joan of Arc." St. Joan Center. Available online at http://www.stjoan-center.com/quotable/.

FURTHER RESOURCES

Discover France
  http://www.discoverfrance.net/France

The French Society
  http://www.understandfrance.org/France/Society/html

Kathleen Kudlinski, *Joan of Arc: A Photographic Story of a Life*. New York: DK Publishing, 2008.

PICTURE CREDITS

INDEX

ABOUT THE AUTHOR

JANET HUBBARD-BROWN has written more than a dozen books for Chelsea House, the majority of them biographies. Jumping from *Joan of Arc* to *Tina Fey* (her other recent biography) was somewhat disorienting, but the author found many similarities in the two women born half a millennium apart—for example, they shared an ironic sense of humor, a strong intelligence, and a self-confidence that allowed them to succeed in a traditionally man's world. A resident of Vermont, Hubbard-Brown works as a writer, editor, and teacher.